Construction EMarketing©

Strategic EMarketing Plans

Researched & Developed by

BRAD FOWLER

CONSTRUCTION EMARKETING ®

Library of Congress Cataloging Number: 2015932384

ISBN 13: 978-0-692-37965-3
ISBN 10: 0692379657

BISAC Subject Headings/ BUS 090010-Business & Economics
BUS 090010-E-commerce/Internet Marketing

Interior cover image from Google.com/images

Printed in the United States of America

CONSTRUCTION EMARKETING ®

P.O. Box 871631
Canton, MI 48187
Email: info@constructionemarketing.biz

About the Author

My academic knowledge and skills in EMarketing were acquired from Capella University Online and Ashford University Forbes School of Business; where I attained a Cum Laude Honorary Bachelor of Arts degree in EMarketing. Currently, I'm completing an Associate of Applied Science degree at Penn Foster College, specializing in Computer Maintenance Technology and a Master of Arts degree specializing in Teaching and Learning with Technology, at Ashford University College of Education. Additionally, I hold a Web site Developer Career Diploma from Penn Foster Career School and a Paralegal Certification from U.S. Career Institute.

I'm an active member of the Internet Marketing Association, New Zealand Marketing Association, Construction Marketing Association, and The Webmaster Association.

"To know wisdom and instruction, to perceive the words of understanding."

-*Proverbs* 1:2

CONTENTS

INTRODUCTION

When I began studying EMarketing, social media marketing, and Internet marketing; instantly, I fell in love with the idea of being able to gain universal computer programming language that would enable me to network with people from all cultural backgrounds, educational levels, religious beliefs, traditions, and countries. And to my surprise, not only has this programming language become the primary element of my career goals and objectives, but aspiring to complete several certifications and degrees in Information Technology, has seemingly enabled me to gain a deeper level of clarity on the importance of the Internet in today's world. In fact, after learning so much about the Internet, Web site designing, and EMarketing, I also discovered the key tools needed to finally unleash my own personal concepts of online marketing, and propel towards a journey that promises no end. After all, the Internet transcends time and delivers an infinite medium of resources.

Furthermore, I also learned a tremendous amount of tech jargon, and the value of various computer software programs such as Adobe®, Apache®, Perl®, Java®, and UNIX®. Learning the importance of each one of these software programs and how to use them effectively and efficiently, as well as having gained knowledge about the construction marketing industry, through course studies and research, over the past five years; has evoked me to put forth more effort to investigate marketing concepts that can best enable those working in the construction marketing industry- to better optimize their Web site development performance and online marketing project deliverance.

And quite honestly, conducting research on the construction marketing industry has also instilled a deeper desire within me- to not only share the resourceful knowledge learned, with those working in the construction marketing industry. Mainly because, the research discovered has enabled me to better define exactly how to approach construction marketing, using today's online technology marketing concepts. After all, in many instances, without this knowledge, it's quite challenging to compete with other tech savvy construction marketers, who are already using every information database in the online environment, to improve their clients' E-business marketability platform.

Shockingly, the tech knowledge and experience gained over the last ten years, also has enabled me to better understand how to efficiently and effectively maximize online advertising budgets, particularly for construction companies seeking to increase their quarterly ROI. However, my quest to understand Internet marketing wasn't the primary reason for studying the construction EMarketing industry. Instead, my quest for clarity rooted deeper after coming to realize the value of EMarketing; the second largest selling product in the United States of America, according to Philip R. Cateora, Mary C. Gilly, and John Graham, authors of International Marketing®.

Therefore, this well-researched construction EMarketing plan, is a new approach to online construction marketing. After all, over the past three years, I've diligently investigated many online construction corporations (large and small) who have been victimized by unqualified online marketing agencies; promising unlimited returns on their investment, while lacking core experience and knowledge about the EMarketing industry and its specialty advertising models. Therefore, to help ease some of the discomfort, you may have about conducting extensive research, I've developed this EMarketing plan; hoping that you will find this data useful and quite helpful as you strive to reach your global EMarketing goals and objectives.

In fact, I recommend using this model as an example, because it enables, you to connect with additional online marketing resources. Besides, using this EMarketing plan will also help your clients' online marketing strategies become better organized, in order to eliminate costly advertising spending, on marketing concepts that will not provide the satisfactory return anticipated. And although there are some differences in the approach towards achieving the same goals and objectives- from one EMarketer to another- the strategies defined within this tool are comprehensive, well researched, and inexpensive to implement.

Take for instance, most traditional marketing plans focus primarily on cultural and economic analysis, market audits, and competitive market analysis. With an EMarketing plan, your initial focus should be on the Situation Analysis, which gives you a forecast of the current issues effecting the growth of your clients' E-business. In addition, is focusing on developing a target market analysis. This is useful because it gives you a firm concept of what audience will be most receptive to benefit from the products, brands and/ or E-commerce services, your client is offering.

Additionally, a great EMarketing plan also focuses on developing a SWOT analysis. This tool deciphers what your clients' E-business strengths are; its weaknesses, opportunities, and threats. Knowing what your clients' E-business strengths are, gives your clients' E-business leverage to redefine its strategy, in order to save the business money and compete with competition. More importantly, a SWOT analysis gives you clarity on your clients' E-business weaknesses. Knowing these intricate details gives your clients' E-business the opportunity to investigate better EMarketing concepts to help eliminate those weaknesses. After all, in many instances, your clients' competitors' are optimizing their online marketing infrastructures completely different. Therefore, having control over your clients' E-business weaknesses, eliminates the negative reputations that can build up online and decrease your clients' E-business value.

Next, a SWOT analysis evaluates the opportunities your clients' E-business has. For instance, construction marketing relies heavily on well researched data from some of today's top online search engines such as Google™, Yahoo™, Bing™, and others. Well, understanding how to utilize these databases and execute a great EMarketing plan, with precision, is what will distinguish your clients' E-business platform from their competitors'. After all, those are your clients' biggest threats. Question is: how do you escape being crushed by the competition?

This is another primary reason for this learning tool's development. To explain who, what, when, where, and how. Who is the competition; what are their motives for their online business practices, when do they drive their most advertising campaign messages towards building better Web site viewer traffic response rates; and how do, they design their EMarketing platform, to continue out ranking your clients' E-business, in global search engine registries.

Furthermore, this plan was developed to share details about the importance of a keyword analysis, which is another intricate part of a search engine query. This primarily deals with terms and words, people use to locate resources online. In fact, if you were to search the keyword-construction, on Google™, the query will return 231,000,000 Web site URL's, in 26 seconds. If you were to search the same keyword on Bing™, you would receive a populated list of 59,400,000. However, on Yahoo™, the search results populates 70,800,000 Web sites; each Web site obviously is seeking to connect with potential consumers, who may be interested in using such business services and/or purchasing products from any one of the listed online resources, other than your client.

This is the great mystery to online marketing: learning how your marketing concepts can compete with millions of other E-Businesses listed in search engines around the world; trying to connect with the same clients' and/or businesses, you and/or your client seeks to connect with. Ideally, this is why using keyword search tools, such as SEO Chat, is essential to your clients' search success; after all, this tool helps your clients' E-business develop better Web pages defined with specific keywords that can be easily woven into the page content of your clients' Web site. In fact, learning how to monopolize this method of design, will give your clients' Web site URL (Uniform Resource Locator) address, prestige in some of the leading top search engines. In fact, Google™ now rates Web sites using SSL (Security Socket Layers) structured with HTTPS- integrated into Web page HTML coding, with higher ranking over those Web sites that typically follow the traditional hypertext markup language: HTTP. Using SSL certificates on your clients' E-business Web pages, adds additional security and separates your clients' E-business Web site from competitors.

In addition, you'll gain understanding on how to develop better Web sites that efficiently promote your clients' E-business. In fact, enclosed are a few Web site design ideas specifically for the construction industry. This is the embodiment of this informative and useful EMarketing plan. Not only have I taken time to develop this insightful tool, with hopes of empowering every construction marketer and/or construction E-business, using the Internet in an attempt to provide clients' with professional, informative, well-researched data. But, I've also invested sincere interest learning what online resources should be considered for implementation, to help construction E-businesses best optimize their online advertising methods.

Therefore, I recommend taking your time and meditating over this information; and then try putting it into practice. And as you work through this tool and begin researching the resources shared, be sure to seek additional resources not discussed. When you do, please be sure to use this EMarketing plan outline as your gateway to building your clients' construction E-business success.

One last thing, when you complete this reading, please share your feedback with me; I might even use your feedback as a blurb in future marketing campaigns to promote this valuable EMarketing tool. You can do so by sending your feedback to: info@constructionemarketing.biz. And please, be sure to put: FEEDBACK, in the subject box of the email. Thank you.

Executive Summary

The E-commerce marketplace continues to evolve into an international gateway of unlimited financial resources and earning potential. Yet in order to achieve financial success with E-commerce, which, both brick & mortar and click & mortar business owners seek to achieve; one must understand the entire perimeter of EMarketing concepts. After all, EMarketing concepts are the most vital component to consider when developing any type of E-business. This means, regardless if the E-business is offering products, services, education, news and/or banking; having a general understanding of EMarketing concepts better enables your clients' business to achieve the success it seeks to achieve through E-commerce.

In fact, in order to completely understand EMarketing concepts, it requires understanding the value of analyzing the proposed target market and the culture of that market. This means, you must also understand that culture's religious beliefs, traditions, rituals, social identities, business ethics, and moral idealisms.

Furthermore, it's imperative to understand your competitors', who are using today's technology on many platforms, which your clients' company may not even have knowledge of, because your clients' business doesn't work closely with a qualified construction EMarketer, who understands today's technology and online marketing strategies. After all, most mainstream Internet marketing gurus, utilize the Internet as a primary source to pin-point new leads, connect with new clients, and establish their clients' brand identity.

But most importantly, your clients' competitors' are using the Internet to build valuable communication with their target audience. Of course, you're probably already aware of this, right? Good. However, quite regrettably, one of the most delicate industries to EMarket, is construction. After all, most land owners and property buyers tend to purchase construction teams, locally. So unless your clients' construction brand image is known and oozes with authority in the industry, especially cyberspace construction sales, your clients' chances of out competing competitors', is almost zero to none. And even if, your client prefers to continue investing millions of dollars in Internet marketing campaigns defined around such marketing concepts as P-P-C (Pay Per Click) banner ads;

then your client may as well open the window and toss their money out for someone else to grab ahold of it, because Pay Per Click banner ads are costly and quite often, do not return on the investment.

This is why building a partnership with a qualified EMarketer, who understands the global construction EMarketing landscape; and who can utilize such skills and knowledge, to help construction marketers' root an online presence in the already congested online construction business environment and begin to flourish. Unlike many other Internet marketers and/or EMarketers', I thrive to offer construction marketers', superior research built on facts. Those facts will enable your clients' E-business to attain the leverage it needs to optimize its online experience.

After all, in order to provide any business with quality service, using top tier technology that gets results, is a must. This is why I stress to all construction marketers'- to think outside the box and redefine what you believe is a well-researched online marketing strategy that brings greater rewards to your clients' company. Most importantly, my EMarketing strategies, will not inspire you to persuade your clients' into investing in dead-end EMarketing concepts that fail. Instead, my EMarketing strategies, render economical EMarketing concepts that lead to long-term business communication alliances, with businesses around the globe. This is why using communication mediums such as Skype®, Webinars, Virtual Conferences, and many other online business environments, will become key components to your clients' E-business success.

Take for instance, Africa and China, both are currently booming in online revenue growth. So much, China now accounts for 44% of all online revenue earnings. While Africa accounts for 33%, according to research compiled by Forrester Research, Inc. Oddly, North America only accounts for 11% of all online sells revenue earned in 2013. Even though, the United States number one selling product is technology. Therefore, it's quite clear that other countries have discovered tremendous value in technology, especially the Internet, more than citizens in the U.S.

Meanwhile, are you aware the Internet accelerates the process of economic growth by speeding up the diffusion of new technologies to emerging economies? Or that, the Internet enables better innovative services at relatively inexpensive cost? Furthermore, are you aware that EMarketing is the critical element in effectively utilizing production resulting from economic growth? And that, EMarketing can define a balance between increased production and increased consumption?

This is why, your clients' E-business must be completely prepared in order to achieve optimal online business success. After all, there are legalities that now infringe upon E-commerce E-businesses, both nationally and internationally. In fact, operating an international E-business requires understanding the legal jurisdiction of conducting E-business in certain countries.

For instance, sending unsolicited emails to Canadian citizens' without prior consent, is against the law in Canada. The recent enacted law defines a thin line between what is considered an ineffective and/or effective legal marketing concept. This new law prohibits emails from outside countries, enveloped with marketing messages that promotes brands. And as odd as this seems, in order to understand why such a law was enacted, its first important to understand the bases for this country's Internet legal systems, which is found in four heritages formed by the majority of the legal systems of the world:

- *Common law, derived from English law and found in England, the U.S., Canada, and other countries under English influence*

- *Civil or code law, which is derived from Roman law and found in Germany, Japan, France, and non-Islamic and non-Marxist countries*
- *Islamic law, which derives from the interpretation of the Koran and found in Pakistan, Iran, Saudi Arabia, and other Islamic states*
- *A commercial legal system in the Marxist-socialist economies of Russia, and the republic of the former Soviet Union, Eastern Europe, China, and other Marxist socialist states, whose legal systems centered on the economic, political, and social policies of the state*

Then there's jurisdiction in international legal disputes and international dispute resolutions, to be concerned with. After all, over the years, these resolutions have become valuable, because page content relevancy on Web sites, now evokes page content thievery. Sadly, many online users tend to ignore intellectual property rights, and copy page content from Web sites, without concern for the Web site owner's property rights.

Take for instance, in some countries, copy written page content, remains up for grabs by page content hackers, who copy and paste E-business Web site page content, into their own Web sites, as a method of stealing another E-business Web site traffic flow or search engine positioning. Of course, this can make your clients' Web site organic search optimization hazardous. Solely because, page content hi-jacking, is prevalent. After all, counterfeit and pirated goods are shipping from a wide range of industries-apparel, automobile parts, agricultural, chemicals, pharmaceuticals, books, records, computer software, mobile phones, baby formula, auto parts, and even cars themselves.

Meanwhile, there are also international differences of language, religion, politics, socialism, values, and ethics that an E- business owner must consider when launching an online marketing campaign. After all, attempting to reach a global market using a single domain name(Web address) for a single, one language Web site, is not what a successful E-business should do, if it's trying to increase its online value.

These are just a few reasons: Why joining forces with a qualified accredited construction EMarketer, is essential to the growth of your clients' E-business success. So to help me convey this rich data, I've compiled scholarly reviewed sources from, both marketing industry leaders, such as Forrester Research, Inc., Internet Retailer Magazine®, Web site Magazine®, Target Market Magazine®, eMarketing.com, and International Construction Magazine®. And additional resources from various marketing data directories, to support this strategic outline; in order for you to better understand: Why EMarketing is a new frontier in the search for alternative ROI earnings in cyber business.

PRODUCT INTRODUCTION

Simply put, construction EMarketing, is online marketing whether via Web sites, online classified ads, opt-in e-mails, interactive kiosks, interactive WebTV, mobile phone ads, social media networking and/or online press release dissemination. In fact, construction EMarketing involves getting closer to businesses and consumers, understanding them better and maintaining a long-term dialogue with them. It is broader than E-commerce since it is not limited to transactions between an organization and its stake- holders, but includes all processes relating to marketing. [1]

In addition, construction EMarketing helps create a business platform that is business 2 business (B2B) led . . . where the E-business owner personally participates – through a constant dialogue, a dynamic dialogue, expressing interests, requesting products and services, suggesting improvements, giving feedback . . . where ultimately, the E-business owner drives the business. In fact, partnering EMarketing with any E- business platform, is a beneficial component to that E-business success, both currently and futuristically. To be exact, below are a few of those benefits:

- Increases sales (through wider distribution of promotional EMarketing campaigns)
- Adds value to the overall business infrastructure and enables a business to build better bridges with consumers, through the offer of extra benefits, such as discounts and takeaways, just for making online purchases
- Brings your clients' closer to other E-businesses, by analyzing the online behavior of prospective clients', asking questions about their likes and dislikes, and actually creating an open dialogue, with industry driven page content, in order to learn more about who your clients' E-business is developing social media network 'Likes' with, so your clients' can better understand how to connect with their target market audience, through the use of social media tools

- Saves cost (of promotions, sales transactions and administration, print and postage) and possibly increases profits on all transactions
- Extends a brands identity and reinforces brand quality and value, with innovative tech driven marketing concepts

Construction EMarketing also includes optimizing search engines, in each and every country, by adding extended country domain names, to fit each countries search engine registry. For instance, using several extended country domain names, such as (www.globalconstruction.com.ca) (Canada), (www.globalconstruction.com.jp) (Japan) or (www.globalconstruction.com.cn) (China), will boost your clients' online strategic EMarketing optimization. After all, with more than 100 countries now utilizing the Internet, having extended domain registered URL's gives your clients' E-business leverage over competitors'.

Even more interesting are top level industry domain names, such as .info, .biz, .construction, .metals, etc. Another reason, why implementing this method of search engine optimization, is so valuable. After all, it enables an E-business to gain additional leads and build better Web site analytics, used to understand what countries are most responsive to industry led search engine queries. Furthermore, utilizing this method of organic search, with country extended domain names correlating with general industry listings, world-wide; and then, implementing the use of a companion Web site that conveys your clients' E-business in various languages, primarily used by your clients' target market; and weaving cultural related graphic art designs onto Web site Web pages that resonate traditional idealisms, will give your clients' additional leverage over competitors'. But be sure to use high resolution, glossy .jpeg, .gif, and .png images. Because using these images correctly and assuring they're measured precisely, with the use of the computer's settings for picture formats, separates your clients' Web site Web pages, from competitors. I say this, because if you've ever landed on a Web site and the upload timing was slow, it has a great deal to do with the lack of professional editing of the embedded graphic images.

Moreover, it's important to understand the intellectual property laws currently protecting the use of some online images being used for commercial use, provided by image database (www.Google.com/images). Using (www.Google.com/images) as a primary resource of imagery for your clients' Web site development, is common because countless other Web site developers are using this search engine to compile images for their clients' Web sites. But recently, I learned that using Google.com/images for commercial use, without permission from Google™, can result in a legal complaint filed against your clients' E-business. Even though, in many instances, such complaints often result in Web site owners receiving "Cease and dismiss" letters, from attorneys, of the Web site owners, where such images were copied from.

However, to combat this, I recommend using resources outside of the country. In fact, one great place I found for free commercial use images, is (www.freeimages.com.uk). This portal of vivid imagery, is packed with loads of free images any U.S. commercial Web site can use for commercial use, without cost.

Moreover, construction EMarketing enables E-businesses to disseminate digital multimedia commercials, more effectively, through the use of Podcast®, YouTube®, Viemo®, Open film®, Motion Box®, and Exposure Room®. This concept of construction EMarketing helps construction E-businesses attain higher viewer response, while also offers a splendid way to conduct better surveys to track Web site viewer response rates. Ideally, having this data helps increase your clients' E-business opportunities and to share intricate details about the company, what the mission of the company is and/or how the company can be of use to another business interested in some of the services your clients' E-business is offering. After all, each time a business uploads a digital multimedia to any one of the above mentioned multimedia broadcasting networks, it increases its chances of building a following that can eventually lead to global business alliances.

Construction EMarketing also includes channeling marketing strategies into well-defined stepping stones that bridge the gap between business to business (B2B) and business to consumers (B2C). Of course, these are just a few primary elements of construction EMarketing concepts, your clients' global construction company should consider implementing, if seeking to become a global online E-business pioneer. After all, construction EMarketing, is a distinguished promotional and marketing concept that impacts consumer and businesses online purchasing decisions; and possesses the power to improve an E-business's return on investment (ROI). Clearly, the obvious benefits of utilizing construction EMarketing to increase your clients' business globally, out weights any traditional marketing concept, your clients' E- business may have already considered implementing.

In fact, construction EMarketing concepts, includes the four S approach: selling, serving, speaking, and saving. Looking at Table 1.1 below, gives you clarity on each of the benefits each (S) component provides.

Table 1.1

Benefits of EMarketing	Transmission of Benefits	Normal Objectives
Selling to Increase Sales	Attained via a wider range of distribution, which isn't economically available offline.	Acquire 10% sales growth in 1-3 years; and 20% sales for each additional product and/or service, in 5 years.
Serving to Add Value	Attained through online surveys, offering consumers' better pricing advantages; providing interesting page content that roots on-going dialogue, which evokes consumers' to share their interest and offer feedback, in order for the EMarketer's to better define e-marketing strategies., to out compete a competitors' EMarketing plans.	Increase global interaction by 10%; increase visitor Web site analysis time frames by 15%; and, to increase the monthly number of consumers', who will become loyal customers' by 20%.

Speaking and Developing Improved Communication with Consumers'	Defining a two-way line of active dialogue between B2B and / or B2C. Utilizing web forms, opt-in and opt-out forms, integrating surveys that ask pertinent questions such as email address, favorite colors, how often the Web site viewer uses online to purchase services and/or to order products the consumer might be interested in learning about and/or purchasing.	Improves email distribution by 25%, with the use of resources from credit bureaus, who provide consumer analytics, both demographically and geographically. Surveying up to 2000 customers' monthly, to increase clarity on consumer needs. Increases search engine ratings by 50%, within the first two years, of implementing a well-defined EMarketing operation.
Save Marketing Cost	Helps reduce the need of staff, printing and postage cost, and reduces cost of direct marketing.	Generates more leads that result with increased sales margins and increased brand awareness, through less expensive marketing concepts.

However, defining these construction EMarketing components for global construction companies, desiring to increase their digital visual experience for their Web site viewers, who are professional business owners, real estate owners, and land owners; knowing what to convey on your clients' Web site to evoke viewers to follow through with each click and make firm E-business negotiations, without physical connectivity, is the challenge in defining a successful strategic construction EMarketing plan. This is why, I like to map out a SOSTAC. After all, it provides clarity on the pertinent data needed to better define a construction EMarketing plan approach, such as focusing on the business situation analysis, strengths, opportunities, strategies, task, actions, and control.

But particularly, for global construction companies operating E-businesses that target such countries as Africa, China, Europe, Latin America, U.K., and Mexico, construction EMarketing has become the essential marketing gateway to help construction E-businesses, weed through the congestion of Internet traffic and search engine build up; and become better defined by key word search queries, that can be, both long-tail or short-tail phrases, consumers and business owners, often use around the globe.

In fact, since there are more than two-hundred top ranking global construction companies on the International Construction company list; and currently, three global construction companies on Forbes® list of the world's biggest public companies, knowing how to monopolize the Internet to win construction contracts and outbid competitors', is again, why construction EMarketer, is valuable to your clients' long-term E-business success. Besides, what is the sense of having a Web site and E-business, if your clients' are not trying to improve their overall online business platform success?

Surely, as a construction marketer, you've come to a point in your search for answers on how to best position your clients' brand online, in order to attain an upper hand over competitors', who seem to be performing much better than your clients' E-business. After all, just looking through some of the top brand name search engines, you can identify who your clients' competitors' are. Clearly, as you can see, you have your work cut out for you. So, I hope this informative plan gives you some light at the end of that dark tunnel, you've been consumed by.

SITUATION ANALYSIS

The congestion of today's global construction marketplace continues to force E-business construction companies to wade through competitive tides of contract bidding and real estate buying wars. To the point, Web analytics needs to be better implemented in order for construction E-businesses to gain greater understanding on the current situations effecting the growth and development of their online E-business marketing environment. Take for instance, Silverstein Properties™, the privately-held, full-service real estate develop, investment, and management firm based in New York; has recently proposed to use construction technology to build the tallest residential building in New York City. The proposed 520 West, 41st Street, property, will encase 1400 apartments, retail, corporate apartments, and 240 low-cost apartments. From my observation, Silverstein Properties™ utilizes its current Web site, to share details about its plans to establish business in China, Israel, and Poland. Yet with so many different global construction companies now targeting countries like China and Africa, exactly how efficient should EMarketing concepts be, in order to win construction contract bids in the online marketplace in those countries?

After all, recently in an article titled *In Africa, U.S. Businesses Are Losing out to China*, I learned that no country in Africa is now untouched by a growing Chinese commercial presence. At the government level throughout the continent, Chinese architecture is sprouting up like mushrooms in a spring forest. It seems as though, in every African capital and major city, the new government buildings are constructed by the Chinese.[2] Furthermore, I learned that a true partnership between the public and private sector, needs to make necessary adjustments to support U.S. investments in Africa, but without leadership, it seems almost impossible to explain to America- the importance of Africa's own economy and political future. Clearly, China's dominance is a growing concern in the United States, especially if U.S. construction companies want to compete in the same countries as China.

As a result, most U.S. companies seeking to compete against the Chinese in countries such as Africa, will need to find financing, pull together a group of companies to do other aspects of the proposed package, such as license registry to operate in foreign territories; and then, try to coordinate those various entities into Africa's business environment. And even if financing were attainable, the African enterprise and government system currently in place, simply is not structured to compete in this manner. Given this reality, American companies are reluctant to compete or as they see it, waste time bidding on contracts, they do not believe they can win.

This is what a construction-EMarketer does; enable construction E-business companies to decipher what resources online are conducive to the needs of the company, and to better convey how to utilize those resources to leverage itself in a new environment that seeks its services. Despite philosophical believes about a nationality of people, a culture, and a belief structure defined by differences in ethics within such cultures, operating a construction E-business can be profitable, with a consistent focus on researching resources in other countries; not just Africa and China, but top ten English speaking countries.

Besides, why would any business purposely impose restrictions upon the marketability of its E-business operations, especially when the Internet freely disseminates portals of databases that are user friendly and accessible 24 hours a day? Surely, setting precedence on new objectives within the digital technology construction marketplace, must be top priority of all construction-EMarketers'. So unless you know what you're doing in this industry, your chances of success may be less attainable than so, if you possessed the key ingredients buried within the endless host of resources in each countries' search engine databases; perfectly organized by industry, and awaiting for U.S. construction E-businesses to connect and make effective business decisions that will enrich not only the lives of families in the U.S., but internationally.

OBJECTIVES

Given the obvious climate of global construction E-business in China and Africa; seemingly, in order for a U.S. construction E-business to reach a global expansion and increase its digital visual display, that evokes contractors to overlook competitors' from countries such as China and others' and actually accept bids from U.S. construction companies; U.S. construction E-businesses need to thrive on the opportunities the EMarketing industry can offer. After all, EMarketers help these E-businesses better understand the facts about their competitors', especially in the digital technology age. Furthermore, an EMarketer enables a company to investigate tactics and marketing strategies, competitors' are implementing around the world. EMarketers also allows construction E-businesses to better prepare their approach to contract bids.

In fact, using online resources such as (www.euromonitor.com), who reports on international trade and marketing; (www.worldchambers.com), who list global businesses; (www. world.wtca.org), which provides extensive details on export assistance, trade leads, and trade missions, as well as (www.worldtrademag.com), who provides guidance on products, goods, services for international trade, and global construction companies; your clients' construction E-business can begin better optimizing the Internet for greater success. However, these resources are just a tip of the iceberg when looking at EMarketing platforms on a global scale in the construction E-business industry.

Today, there are more than 20 countries actively using the Internet to conduct everyday business. And those 20 countries offer more than 23 million estimated registered URL's in their search engines. So, how can anyone find your clients' construction E- business, without having a mediator moderate the connection through strategic EMarketing concepts? Honestly, it would seem almost impossible to achieve. Therefore, in order to become more successful at competing in the online construction EMarketing environment, construction-marketers need to build their skills and roll up their sleeves, in order to dig deep within the files of database research that remains untouched.

Let's face it, the EMarketing platform doesn't change no matter what industry it is. What I've come to understand does change, is the marketing platform for the construction E-business industry, because it stands on the values of an E-businesses online reputation. Therefore, building better EMarketing objectives that help meet the company's goals- quarterly; requires, conducting thorough analysis on the outcome of previous, present, and future online marketing practices used in your clients' online marketing strategies. After all, doing so better prepares your clients' to win bigger bids, with every approach, every time.

STRATEGIES

Utilizing online resources such as those mentioned in the previous segment of this construction-EMarketing plan, not only provides helpful insight on how to out-source competitors' in a global market, but enables a construction E-business, working in China, Africa, Europe, United States and/or Mexico, to win better performance ratings and build stronger metrics that best explains how to continue winning in the construction E-business marketplace. Take for instance, (www.jetro.go.jp/usa), is an online resource Web site providing companies' intelligent data that connects them with scheduled meetings on construction industry issues, such as real estate development conferences held around the U.S.

Interestingly, this Japan External Trade Organization, offers its Web site data in different languages, hoping to share continued vital news about business transactions, with construction companies working in a global environment. This is a great place for Construction E-businesses to network, advertise, and gain additional leverage over competitors'.

Then, there's also (www.export.gov/tradeleads/), which the U.S. government uses to share resources internationally, in Embassies and Consulates that help identify promising leads for U.S. exporters. This dynamic database can be utilized to increase knowledge on how to approach foreign leads and win contract bids. However, only a qualified well informed construction EMarketer possesses the know how to effectively identify such leads and/or how to define better online research that can "almost" guarantee a construction E-business, global marketing expansion, leading to global business alliances.

TACTICS

As mentioned previously, using Web site design platforms developed with professional style and appeal, and offering in-depth, relevant data (page content) on the Web site Web pages, about the company, is the first tactic that must be implemented to not only draw Web site viewers, but increase viewer feedback response rates. In fact, a professional construction E-business Web site should be:

a. *Well-written and offer informative page content that evokes interest in what the company is offering; its achievements, objectives, and goals.*
b. *Developed with digital multimedia embedded in, both the index.html homepage and the "About" and "Services", Web pages, because this gives Web site viewers an impersonal connection with the company.*
c. *Designed with high resolution graphic images that complement page content; and have relevancy to the overall theme of the Web site.*

d. *Built with Opt-in and Opt-out, feedback, and contact us forms. Surveys should also be added as often as possible to increase the company's insight on what Web site viewers are seeking from the company.*
e. *Use online construction industry and construction E-business magazine Web sites, to share news stories; analyze competitors' press release news, and target, with news about successes your clients' construction E-business has and/or is planning to achieve, is another tactic practiced in beating competitors' and winning construction E-business contracts and bids in cyberspace.*
f. *Implement digital multimedia commercials that convey a universal marketing message, targeted towards the top three professional business languages; and disseminating such commercials to international news networks and global online community newsletters; in order to better monopolize international business networking group Web sites, such as LinkedIn™, Facebook™, Twitter™, aSmallWorld™, Asian Avenue™, Biip.no™; and the business executive social media*

Web site, Elixio™, which caters to the jet set global elite.

These are just a few social media networks to consider utilizing when EMarketing a construction E-business, globally. But these are not the sole mediums to focus on. As pointed out before, using all country search engine databases, by industry search query, gives you a better range of data to comb through and position your clients' construction E-business, with a systematic treasure of business to business information. In fact, one information portal I recently found quite insightful for the international construction industry, can be accessed at (http://construction.com/dodge/). This platform helps position your clients' search for contract bidding.

Another portal I found useful, is (http://www.bidocean.com/freebidleads.php). This information database offers national and international bid lead services. In addition, it offers state bidding networks and additional North American "free" bidding Web site links. To me, this is the joy of construction EMarketing: utilizing the 17,000,000,000 Web sites populated in a given search query, to grow and develop a clients' online marketing presence.

ACTIONS

This is why action plans should be concrete and executed with precision. This means, narrowing down top competitors' and out sourcing them with Internet based marketing and networking tools, as mentioned previously. This generally includes: obtaining essential data analytics that provides quality insight on competitors' past, present, and future proposed business developments. Plus, utilizing industry data bases such as (www.theconstructionindex.co.uk/), as a catalyst, enables your clients' construction E-business to reap full benefits beyond its competitors' online marketing actions and tactics, because this database provides contract leads, international construction news, construction features, such as health and safety, structural steel work sector, demolition, flood protection , piling and ground engineering, road utilities and street work, scaffolding and access, and cladding and insulation.

Using such online E-business tools effectively and efficiently, helps your clients' construction E-business better strategies against those competitors' taking full advantage of these informative and useful online marketability platforms. One reason why, I cannot stress enough: the importance of not ignoring the countless number of resources available online in one database or another. After all, neglecting to monopolize databases can lead to weak points in your clients' online marketing opposition and/or their ability to compete against competitors' overall EMarketing concepts and strategies.

In fact, optimizing online legal business news databases, such as Lexis Nexis™, the National Law Review™, Corporate Law Report™, and others, who convey in-depth legal information and research about businesses legal disputes and current enacted laws, both nationally and internationally, helps determine what competitors' have been up to and/or are planning to achieve in coming years. So knowing how to use these databases to obtain news worthy data about competitors', enables your clients' construction E-business to adapt and/or revise its EMarketing strategies in compliance with competitors'.

Take for instance, in a recent article on Corporate Loss Due To Poor Communication, I learned that poor communication can be more than a common cause of frustration for employees and employers. In fact, it can cause a range of negative consequences for a corporation.

Barriers to effective communication include choosing the wrong medium for message delivery, overuse of complicated jargon, and failing to understand the role emotions play in a message's acceptance. One of the most dangerous aspects of poor communication, as well as one of the most overlooked, is failing to listen.[3]

Furthermore, in another article titled *The Construction Industry's Ethical Dilemma* authored by Ellen Parson, I learned that, Dennis Doran, FMI Market Manager, owner services, set out to examine in the "Survey of Construction Industry Ethical Practices," a recent study that takes an in-depth look at ethics in the construction industry. According to Parson, Doran prepared the anonymous online survey and conducted it in conjunction with the Construction Management Association of America, which sent out the questionnaire electronically to its membership, in an effort to gauge ethical practices and concerns in the industry. Additional research also proved The American Subcontractors Association did the same, offering its members a link through the organization's Web site to help solicit feedback.[4] Parson added, that since corporate financial scandals have become more commonplace, Doran notes that whole industries have come under suspicion, prompting the creation of the

Sarbanes-Oxley Act, which was signed into law, in July 2002, by President Bush, to protect investors by improving the accuracy and reliability of corporate disclosures. Breaches in construction ethics have a price, but according to Parson, Doran conveys that focusing too much on financial fallout may contribute to the public's misunderstanding of the concept.

Hypothetically, when a lot of people think about ethics, they automatically go to a simple notion of what brought about Sarbanes-Oxley — financial impropriety, improper reporting of financial revenues, and things with a primary focus on public companies. But like Parson says, Doran believes, ethics is more than just reporting financial results incorrectly. Instead, ethics is an issue of extreme importance to most people working in the construction industry, but at the same time, it remains an issue no one wants to talk about publicly.

In fact, ethics remains questionable not only in the construction industry, but there have also been ethic issues in the EMarketing industry. Take for instance, online marketing activities can offer a lot of opportunities for companies to uniquely market themselves and their products, inexpensively and effectively. Yet in order to do so, companies need to exercise considerable care to ensure their methods of EMarketing, do not get them into legal difficulties. After all, consumer concerns about unethical practices on the Internet are directly about having an effect on the take up of electronic commerce as well as EMarketing platforms. Therefore, while many people are willing to access the Internet to conduct business, both personally and professionally, there still are countless consumers and business owners who lack trust in some online businesses, which prevents many businesses from optimizing the Internet and its unlimited resources, to save money and attain the income growth they seek.

Ideally, unethical behavior also includes actions that result in unfairness to others, whether those behaviors' are legal or not. Unethical actions can be aimed towards competitors. Businesses will attempt to win customers away from competing businesses, as fair competition is a cornerstone to a free enterprise economy.[5] Furthermore, previous research also indicated that unethical practices in EMarketing has established a key barrier to the use of Internet shopping as well as intruding upon the development of long-term customer loyalty.

So as the number of people using the Internet to shop continues to steadily rise, a number of Laws and Regulations agencies are being constructed simultaneously;

namely: FTC and COPAA, which controls EMarketing ethics. Still, even though such organizations exist, there are many electronic- marketing concepts that are considered to be crossing over E-business ethical boundaries. Surely, this, too, meets the current climate in unethical performances of construction E-business marketing practices.

In fact, current data research conveys that unethical performance is an impediment for economic development and good governance. It is more than true to say it is the bane of development in developing nations of the world under which Nigeria is categorized. Oddly, there, the construction sector was highlighted for its practices in areas such as bribery, environmental destruction, capital flight, dangerous practices, poor quality, whistle blowing, etc.; and it is also associated with unethical behavior, through the entire construction life cycle.[6]

Therefore, it is important to instill viable legislation as a mechanism to dealing with small levels of corruption through the strengthening of professional institutions that punish erring members. However, this will only prevent corruption to a certain degree; while enabling E-businesses to implement security enforcement and monitoring measures being recommended by such anti-corruption agencies. As a result, this creates an enabling environment possible for the construction EMarketing industry to thrive, operate, and improve quality and quantity of infrastructure on a more sustainable basis; and thereby, foster good construction EMarketing ethics, in the long run.

Again this is another reason why it's so important to understand how to combat your clients' online competitors'. After all, this correlates with another action in corporate construction EMarketing concepts, which includes: investigating competitors' Web site performances and EMarketing strategies. In fact, one way to begin this journey, is by researching TLD'S (Top-level domains), which is the rightmost part of a domain name.

Interestingly, the Internet Corporation for Assigned Names and Numbers (ICANN) has the responsibility of populating and managing domain names and matching them with IP addresses. As a result, in 2000, ICANN added seven new TLD's, including the following: (.biz, .info, .name, and .pro).[7] Meanwhile, additional TLD's have been added since 2000; and ironically, some of those TLD's are designed to correlate with different countries as pointed out previously.

In fact, looking at Table 1.2, you can learn some of the most important and frequently used TLDs'.

Table 1.2

Original Generic TLD's	Generic TLD's added in 2000	Country TLD's
TLD USE	TLD USE	TLD USE
.com U.S. commercial	.uk United Kingdom	.au Australia
.edu U.S. four-year educational institution	.asia Companies, individuals, and organizations based in Asia-Pacific regions	.ca Canada
.gov U.S. federal government	.biz Businesses	.de Germany
.mil U.S. Military	.info General use	.fi Finland
.net U.S. general use	.int International organization and programs endorsed by a treaty between or among nations	.fr France

.org U.S. not-for profit organization	.name Individual persons	.jp Japan
.us U.S. general use	.pro Professionals (lawyers, Doctors and accountants)	.se Sweden

Data compiled from Electronic Ecommerce, 8th Ed: top-level domain names

The next valuable action, is knowing how to combat domain hi-jacking, which unfortunately continues to become a growing problem year after year. Despite this fact, increased consumer anti-phishing awareness and improved anti-spam technologies have gradually reduced the impact of traditional phishing spams in recent years. So to keep up their game in a multi-billion dollar cybercrime industry, hackers have been continuously innovative in developing polymorphic phishing channels. Spear phishing, malware, search engine poisoning, use of rogue Secure Socket Layer (SSL) certificates, mobile and social media attacks are among the modern and prominent channels for phishing attacks today.[8]

Furthermore, many disputes regarding domain name resolutions exist, both privately and officially. So much, most of the Alternative Dispute Resolution (ADR) systems adopted, largely rest upon the Uniform Domain Name

Dispute Resolution Policy (UDRP), which is already established and has gained a respectable track record. Because of this, some jurisdictions have adopted the UDRP completely in spite of its narrow scope. Others have preferred to extend the range of distinguishing signs protected and have adopted extended versions of UDRP. For instance, a third group of countries has sense developed their own "*sui generis*" (unique class all alone) ADRs that are unconnected to the UDRP. Oddly, the most distinctive characteristic of all ADR examples analyzed, is the availability of a twofold procedure due to their "open ended" nature.

Meanwhile, some jurisdictions have adopted classic arbitration procedures for their domain name disputes, which result with final judgments enveloped with *res judicata* effect. As regards substantive grounds of claim, there is also a large variety of approaches. Notably, most of the European countries prefer to extract the bases of anti-cybersquatting claims from general laws regarding trademarks, unfair completion, passing off of personal and trade name protection.[9]

Certainly, implementing strategic EMarketing concepts that help combat such terroristic acts as cybersquatting and/or domain hijacking, deserves investigating, in order to better understand what your clients' construction E-business is up against. But more importantly, taking action to gain the knowledge to better understand what steps your clients' construction E-business should take to avoid being victimized cannot be ignored.

Another action to focus on is the Web site design platform and performance of your clients' construction E-business. After all, currently, the top five countries ranking by average E-commerce sales per online shopper, with their 2012 and 2013 projected averages, were:

- United Kingdom, $3,585, $3,878;
- Australia, $3,547, $3,802;
- Norway, $2,530, $2,796;
- United States, $2,293, $2,466;
- Denmark, $2,185, $2,286.

However, in 2013, E-commerce sales in China accounted for 14% of all online sales worldwide; reaching $181.62 billion, up 65% from $110.04 billion, in 2012. The United States in 2013 took 29.6% of all online sales and/ or $384.80 billion, up 12.2% from $343.43 billion in 2012.[10] And although, China seems to be beating other markets in E-commerce revenue earnings, based on the size of its online shopping population, the average Chinese shopper is estimated to spend only $670 online in 2015, according to an article titled Top Online Sellers in 2015, in the pages of Internet Retailer®, the print medium magazine to E-commerce intelligence. In contrast, online shoppers in the United Kingdom, were estimated to spend an average of $3,878 each in 2015, up from $3,585 per shopper in 2012, when it took the global lead for highest average E-commerce spending per shopper. So when considering the total number of registered domain names in search engines, globally, which today accounts for an estimated 1 billion registered Web site names; it's not easy ranking number one on top search engine listings.

In fact, examining Table 1.3 below, gives you a more in-depth look into this dynamic analysis.

Table 1.3

Year	Websites	Chang	Internet Users	Users per Website	Websites launched
2013	**672,985,183**	-3%	2,756,198,420	4	
2012	**697,089,489**	101%	2,518,453,530	4	
2011	**346,004,403**	67%	2,282,955,130	7	
2010	**206,956,723**	-13%	2,045,865,660	10	Pinterest

2009	**238,027,855**	38%	1,766,206,240	7	
2008	**172,338,726**	41%	1,571,601,630	9	Dropbox
2007	**121,892,559**	43%	1,373,327,790	11	Tumblr
2006	**85,507,314**	32%	1,160,335,280	14	Twitter
2005	**64,780,617**	26%	1,027,580,990	16	YouTube, Reddit
2004	**51,611,646**	26%	910,060,180	18	The Facebook, Flickr
2003	**40,912,332**	6%	778,555,680	19	WordPress, LinkedIn
2002	**38,760,373**	32%	662,663,600	17	
2001	**29,254,370**	71%	500,609,240	17	Wikipedia
2000	**17,087,182**	438%	413,425,190	24	Baidu
1999	**3,177,453**	32%	280,866,670	88	PayPal
1998	**2,410,067**	116%	188,023,930	78	Google
1997	**1,117,255**	334%	120,758,310	108	Yandex
1996	**257,601**	996%	77,433,860	301	
1995	**23,500**	758%	44,838,900	1,908	AltaVista, Amazon, Auction Web
1994	**2,738**	2006%	25,454,590	9,297	Yahoo
1993	**130**	1200%	14,161,570	108,935	
1992	**10**	900%			
Aug. 1991	**1**				World Wide Web Project

Source: ***Net Craft and Internet Live Stats*** (elaboration of data by *Matthew Gray of MIT and Hobbes' Internet Timeline* and *Pingdom)*

As mentioned previously, today we are rapidly approaching 1 billion registered Web sites; a milestone, which will be reached by the end of 2015. Just imagine, the Internet grew from 1 Web site in 1991 to over 700 million, in 2013; the chart and table above shows the total number of Web sites registered by year throughout history. Of course, let me clarify what I mean by Web site; this primarily means: unique hostname (a name which can be resolved, using a name server, into an IP Address). Please note that around 75% of Web sites today are not active, but have parked domains or similar.[11]

Meanwhile, periodic drops in the total count of Web sites; seemingly, depends on various factors, including an improvement in Net Craft's (www.news.netcraft.com) handling of wildcard hostnames. This is useful because Net Craft provides great Internet research, anti-phishing, data mining, and security testing. For example, in August 2012, over 40 million hostnames on only 242 IP addresses were removed from the Survey. Therefore, considering there are so many Web sites already registered, how effective do you think a construction EMarketing plan should be, in order to combat the online marketing plans of countless other construction E-business Web sites, competing for the same business? Clearly, the outcome to construction-

EMarketing success depends solely upon the construction-EMarketer's research strategies. In fact, in order to be effective in this game, construction E-business owners must join forces with skilled and educated EMarketers', who understand Web site development and, who possesses the intelligence to not only define a Web site that offers viewers superior functionality, but meets today's ISO (International Standard Organization) professional Web site standards. If not, your clients' Web site could end up on: Web Pages That Suck (www.webpagesthatsuck.com), a Web site that analyzes Web sites and Web site performances.

After all, there are many facets to defining Web sites that welcome viewers with valuable page content offering real researched data worth reading. Take for instance, today's Web site viewers do not have time to waste reading a full Web page of data. Instead, Web site viewers want instant data, with little inconvenience. This is why it's important to build an organic search engine plan. Research conveys that when seeking any given E-Business industry, the majority of U.S. Internet users turn to Google®, Yahoo® and/or Bing®; and enter keywords such as those mentioned previously.

Surprisingly, the number of Web page search results often turns out a response rate of more than 4,419,000,000 Web sites to search through in order to decipher which Web sites are most valuable. Unfortunately, for those Web sites listed beyond the fourth page, as mentioned before, many Web site viewers vaguely ever get the opportunity to search beyond Web site surface Web pages. This is because most Web site viewers will not research Web pages beyond the 3rd or 4th page, during any given search.

Clearly, from these facts, it's quite easy to understand the total number of resources that continues to go untouched by Web site viewers. Shockingly, this untouched data is a driving force that impacts a construction EMarketing campaign. After all, if a construction E-business marketing team were to comb through the populated list of resources found in any given search engine while conducting search engine research, and actually left a trail of comments, along with the construction E-business URL, on newspaper article post, blog post, forum post, and daily Facebook post closely related to current industry news; those construction E-businesses would be leaving a trail of links leading back to their construction E-business Web site.

And since there is often a limited number of characters allotted for use in most online news portal feedback response forms, post are limited to 140 characters. However, to combat this, an informative EMarketer will insert a bit link, which shortens a URL (www.globalconstruction.com) and conveys it as (http://bit.ly/Zj792y). This useful tool can be accessed at (www.bitly.com). Or, you can search for additional URL shorter, by using the following links (www.goo.gl), (tinyurl.com) and/or (www.is.gd).

Additionally, offering a Web site that speaks industry language and invites viewers to share input based on the Web site's page content, is another important tool used to increase viewer response. In fact, below is a compiled history of a few search engines that may be currently active and/or inactive:

Year	Engine	Current status
1993	W3Catalog	Inactive
	Aliweb	Inactive
	JumpStation	Inactive
	WWW Worm	Inactive
1994	WebCrawler	Active, Aggregator

	Go.com	Active, Yahoo Search
	Lycos	Active
	Infoseek	Inactive
	AltaVista	Inactive, redirected to Yahoo!
	Daum	Active
1995	Magellan	Inactive
	Excite	Active
	SAPO	Active
	Yahoo!	Active, Launched as a directory
	Dogpile	Active, Aggregator
1996	Inktomi	Inactive, acquired by Yahoo!
	HotBot	Active (lycos.com)
	Ask Jeeves	Active (rebranded ask.com)
1997	Northern Light	Inactive
	Yandex	Active
	Google	Active
1998	Ixquick	Active also as Start page
	MSN Search	Active as Bing
	empas	Inactive (merged with NATE)
	AlltheWeb	Inactive (URL redirected to Yahoo!)
1999	GenieKnows	Active, rebranded Yellowee.com
	Naver	Active
	Teoma	Inactive, redirects to Ask.com
	Vivisimo	Inactive
	Baidu	Active
2000	Exalead	Active
	Gigablast	Active
2003	Info.com	Active

	Scroogle	Inactive
2004	Yahoo! Search	Active, Launched own web search (see Yahoo! Directory, 1995)
	A9.com	Inactive
	Sogou	Active
2005	AOL Search	Active
	GoodSearch	Active
	SearchMe	Inactive
2006	wikiseek	Inactive
	Soso (search engine)	Active
	Quaero	Active
	Ask.com	Active
	Live Search	Active as Bing, Launched as rebranded MSN Search
	ChaCha	Active
	Guruji.com	Inactive
2007	wikiseek	Inactive
	Sproose	Inactive
	Wikia Search	Inactive
	Blackle.com	Active, Google Search
2008	Powerset	Inactive (redirects to Bing)
	Picollator	Inactive
	Viewzi	Inactive
	Boogami	Inactive
	LeapFish	Inactive
	Forestle	Inactive (redirects to Ecosia)
	DuckDuckGo	Active

	Bing	Active, Launched as rebranded Live Search
2009	Yebol	Inactive
	Mugurdy	Inactive due to a lack of funding
	Scout (Goby)	Active
	NATE	Active
	Blekko	Active
2010	Cuil	Inactive
	Yandex	Active, Launched global (English) search
2011	YaCy	Active, P2P web search engine
2012	Volunia	Inactive

Data derived from http://en.wikipedia.org/wiki/Web_search_engiee

Using such mediums to register your clients' construction-E-business Web site with, is not enough anymore when trying to defeat competitors in search engine ranking. This is why actions is a vital component in the SOSTAC development. Outlining the actions needed to spearhead a construction E-business EMarketing campaign, requires possessing valuable knowledge and resourceful tools and information that enables a company to meet its objectives and goals, while enabling it to build a positive reputation management image in the eyes of Web site viewers, seeking quality service providers, such as your clients'.

In fact, viewing the above list of search engines; clearly, you can see just how fast some Internet resources become unavailable with the snap of the finger. However, this list doesn't convey all of the global search engines. After all, as mentioned previously, each country has established its own search engines that can be accessed by using that country's TLD's. This is why, I believe learning about such intricate details in the construction EMarketing environment, are so important; after all, understanding these resources can increase your client's ROI, substantially.

CONTROL

Managing control over a Web site's brand identity and visual display, can be a daunting process. Mainly because, unlike small business Web sites that can be designed by using predesigned Web site templates from online mediums such as (www.web.com), (www.lyco.com), and (www.godaddy.com); large E-businesses often implement dynamic Web sites, which require a lot more bells and whistle, higher cost to maintain, and professional control over flexibility. But if you truly desire for your clients' construction E-business to be defined by search engine optimization, it's important to investigate those Web site template platforms, you may decide to use when developing your clients' Web site landscape, because you'll need to query the Web site hosting company to ask if you can integrate Meta tags and keywords in the HTML (Hypertext Markup Language) code. After all, HTML is valuable to the definition and title of Web site's search engine ranking.

Ideally, this technology enables Web site developers' full use of hyperlinks (http ://) on Web site Web pages. This is because, Hyperlinks contain Uniform

Resource Locator (URL), which links one Web page to another and/ or to another Web site's Web page. The URL is simply the Web site name and page.[12] By defining a Web site with HTML coding, a construction E-business Web site integrated with industry base keywords, has a better chance of ranking higher in search engines. After all, keywords are vital, as mentioned before, because they play an intricate role in how your clients' Web sites are listed in search engines and/or how your clients' Web site is discovered in a search engine query. And while some search engine seekers often input single term words, using long-tail and short tail phrases- phrases with four or more terms, increases a search engine seeker's number of Web page responses.

For example, if someone was searching for global construction companies. The long-tail search word used could be: list of global construction companies that have good standing reputations. A short-tail word search could be: global construction. With long-tail keywords, it's much easier to get your target market's attention because there's less competition using long-tail keywords. Most of your competitors' aren't concentrating on this style of keywords, so using them will always will be, your golden egg.[13]

Furthermore, people tend to use long-tail keywords for searches when they're getting close to making a purchase.

Another step in taking control of your clients' construction E-business EMarketing strategies, is implementing industry based communication networks that are consumer orientated. Take for instance, blogging is one of the most effective tools used to share tips and valuable industry news and updates that evoke dialogue between Internet users. Blogging can also be another medium of EMarketing products, services, and/or goods. With a blog your clients' construction E-business can build a list of followers and gain valuable feedback supporters, who may be interested in the E-business Web site page content and provide links to their profile links on social media networks, such as Facebook®, LinkedIn®, and Twitter®. This web of networking enables your clients' construction E-business to connect with the followers' of those following you.

In fact, when using a Facebook® fan page as a medium to promote, sell, and/or provide services, your clients' construction E-business gains an additional list of followers', who actually 'LIKE' their Fan Page, because of the services, products and/ or goods, you as the construction marketer, is marketing. Using this medium of connectivity enables your clients' construction E-business to share vital news and events with Web site viewers that may be happening, both in the immediate and/or near future.

So just imagine, if your clients' Facebook® Fan Page was defined and developed identically to their primary Web site homepage. Each follower that 'Likes' your clients' Fan Page, is now a dependable medium of network that enables you as the construction marketer, to share data about your clients' services, products and/or goods, with those who are joined to their Facebook® pages as well. Therefore, if you post a press release on your clients' Facebook® Fan Page, and you have 2,000 people who have 'Liked' your clients' Fan Page, already; every time you post something, each one of those 2,000 people, gets a copy of what you posted. Now, whatever you post is going to be shared on your followers' (only those who 'Like' you) Facebook® page.

For example, of the 2,000 viewers who have connected with your client; imagine if each had 10 followers' on their Facebook® Web page. Posting one post, is now disseminated to 20,000 people. Therefore, the objective to building a Facebook® Fan Page audience, is driving the number of 'Likes' up so those supporters become primary gateways to additional connectivity sources of online Web site viewers. And since this EMarketing strategy is specifically for the construction industry, building a fan base on Facebook® should include industry related followers' such as construction journalist, construction magazine editors and newspaper editors, for example. These important connections are great leads to building long term alliances that help increase your clients' construction E-business leverage over competitors'.

Furthermore, blogs can also be used to increase feedback responses to surveys about industry news and innovativeness. This can also lead to article marketing. This concept of marketing, is another valuable asset to construction-EMarketing. After all, writing news articles about industry topics and laws associated with the industry, increases a construction E-business Web site traffic. It also helps a construction E-business build a larger reading audience. Take for instance, the Engineering News Record (www.enr.construction.com), is a great medium to share and post response feedback to industry related topics that increases Web site viewer response. Another resource is International Construction, which can be accessed by download via iTunes.[14]

Interestingly, there are more than 150,000,000 search results for the short-tail phrase: global construction news groups. Plus, it's important not to forget, there are also industry blogs such as Mod Space Blog-Construction News, Updates and Insights, or Global Construction Review. There's also the Construction Marketing Association® blog, which recently conducted a national survey of construction professionals. The following questions were asked:

1. How often do you employ social media in your marketing program?

2. If yes, how often do you manage social media marketing internally or outsource?

3. What social media networks do you employ?

4. Do you include blogging?

5. Have you considered utilizing paid advertising?

6. What social media have you learned about that is MOST effective in achieving the best marketing results?

7. What social media network has been LEAST effective in achieving the best marketing results?

Asking such questions helped this association increase its awareness on different social media marketing techniques employed by other construction marketers.

Another important control for your clients' construction-EMarketing plan, is concentrating on your clients' construction E-business social media profiles. In fact, recent studies have shared that- construction businesses are sorely lacking when it comes to social media marketing and similar profit boosting strategies. It's not that they don't have the resources to run a successful campaign – many construction E-business owners simply don't know how important having a social media presence can be. As compared to other industries, the skilled trades have a low participation rate in social media channels – this means there is less 'virtual' competition and that this is the perfect time to launch your social media marketing promotions.[15]

In addition, it's important to understand the value of disseminating honest page content woven into the Web pages of a trust worthy Web site. This is essential, because potential customers and/or businesses want to know they're doing business with a reputable company and real live people. Therefore, adding in-depth profile data on your clients' social media profile links, such as fundraising and sporting events the company has sponsored. Posting images of those events and sharing multimedia with up close and personal interviews, with attendees, also helps increase viewers' interest in your clients' construction E-business profile.

As a result, any construction company operating an E-business store front, should convey the name of the brand, company owner's name, year founded, and the number of successful projects completed, with links opening in new windows, enabling Web site viewers to review magazine and newspaper articles, past and presently written about the company, but not leaving the Web site. The profile should also link to digital multimedia on YouTube®. Using YouTube® and others alike, such as Podcast®, enables you to set a platform to draw Web site viewers interested in the three to five minute multimedia segments, elected to convey additional information about the company.

That being said, please don't make the mistake of not using your clients' construction E-business social media profile as their own personal sounding board. Customers want to know how certain aspects of a business owner and/or employees personal life pertain to the business. For example, having one of the company's professionals (engineer, cementers, managers, etc.), provide details about various projects they've taken an active role in, can be a great way to let potential consumers (business owners) learn more about the company's team players. This is also a great way to enable potential customers' the opportunity to witness such employees express their personal views about certain projects completed. Even venting about a horrible experience, or perhaps going on a tangent about some negative aspect of their personal experiences on a job, will encourage customers' to build a better trust and appreciation for the company.

Meanwhile, it's useful to consider placing banner advertisements on Web sites closely related to your industry and Web site Web page content. Please be aware that banner sizes come in various shapes and sizes, which can be found by conducting a keyword search for: ad banner samples. Doing so will enable you to locate charts that provide Web site ad banner size charts. In fact, using the link below, will give you a general idea (http://en.wikipedia.org/wiki/Web_banner) of the various banner ad sizes in dimension.

Simply adding an ad banner linked to Web sites such as county and city operated Web sites, real estate, mortgage companies, real estate auctions and/or construction apparel brands like Carhartt®; allows your clients' construction E-business to disseminate its brand logo and/or message in additional marketing formats. For example, ad banners are a great way of promoting affiliate marketing campaigns. Ideally, affiliate marketing is a type of performance-based marketing, which a business rewards one or more affiliates, for each visitor or customer brought to the vending location by the affiliate's own marketing efforts. Registering your clients' construction E-business with affiliate marketing Web sites, such as TOP SEO's, who provides a number of EMarketing related industry tools for the U.S., U.K., Australia, India, and world-wide, will positon your clients' E-business on a higher visibility scale. Furthermore, using this medium wisely, will help your clients' construction E-business better connect with Web site viewers, who will ultimately drive traffic to the Web site and increase the percentage of sells transactions that occur via affiliate marketing links, from one Web site to another. Additional affiliate marketing programs will require registering your clients' construction E-business, in a classified industry listing on such Web site as (www.zanox.com/us/). This affiliate marketing portal enables E-commerce product and service providers with the following opportunities:

- *Market products and/or services to a targeted audience and only pay when you get paid*

- *Gain maximum reach via global publisher network with a wide variety of publisher models*

- *Display ads on a Web site and earn money for generating sales and leads*

- *Benefit from their global network of high-quality brands and attractive promotions*

Meanwhile, Web sites such as (www.giveawaytools.com) enables Web site owners to drive growth and build brand recognition, through giveaway tools. By simply configuring the Web site's HTML code and integrating the predesigned web application offered by the company marketing (www.giveawaytools.com), your clients' construction E-business can then begin asking for survey responses and extend promotions and giveaways as incentives. By the way, on (www.giveawaytools.com)registration is absolutely free!

Another tool that's useful can be found on (www.compezy.com), which offers Web site owners effective giveaway campaigns that offer Web site viewers, free gifts. You may think that giving away products or information is going to cost your clients' money and negatively affect their bottom line. Nothing could be further from the truth. People tend to pay attention when they see or hear the word, 'free.' Therefore, when a person sees they're getting something for free, generally, they feel more obligated to engage with the provider of that free offering. This is known as reciprocity, you give to me, and in return, I give to you. So free giveaways actually increase your bottom line, rather than affect it negatively. Offering free giveaways through your clients' construction E-business Web site, is actually one of the most successful marketing techniques being used by your competition today.

Clearly, as you can see, controlling how your EMarketing strategies differ from your clients' competitors', is important. And using mediums such as blogging, article writing, affiliate marketing promotions, and placing ad banners on Web sites closely related to your clients' industry, while offering giveaways on the Web site, are just a few additional tools to consider implementing when defining your clients' construction- EMarketing strategies. This is why it's important to develop a SWOT analysis; after all, this uniquely designed analysis helps a company determine its strengths, weaknesses, opportunities, and threats. Understanding these valuable components and their position to the growth and success of the construction E-business, enables your clients' E-business to better promote itself and establish new online territory for promotional impact, while enabling the E-business to better plan how to execute an efficient EMarketing plan that will continue to position your clients' Web site ranking, higher than their online competition. Learning what strengths, weaknesses, opportunities, and threats your clients' E-business faces, gives your clients' construction E-business leverage to compete with their global competitors'.

Strengths

- **Brand awareness**

1. Having a powerful brand presence online is essential to building brand awareness. This can include having ad banners, click through links attached to a company logo placed on an industry related Web site, as well as offering marketing tools to increase awareness of your clients' company existence. Ideally, such marketing tools can also include: custom designed t-shirts, bags, coffee

mugs, ink pens, and other items alike. You can find a great selection of promotional marketing tools on such Web sites such as (www.zazzle.com), (www.cafepress.com), or (www.vistaprint.com).

2. Offering Web site viewers a companion Web site in different languages, such as Spanish, is another strength your clients' E-business can adapt and integrate into its online marketing strategies. After all, doing so broadens your clients' online promotional efforts and increases brand awareness, with Spanish speaking countries and cultures. In fact, formatting the companion Web site with Spanish culture tradition colors and images, helps Web site viewers from Spanish speaking countries, better connect with E-business marketing platforms in a language the Web site viewer is comfortable reading.

3. Sharing news about awards received, newspaper articles that convey positive comments about the success of any projects completed; of course, are additional key tools used to build brand awareness.

4. It's also important to keep in mind that your clients' E-business strengths will differ greatly from

their competitors', from time to time. This is why it's essential to conduct thorough research on your clients' competitors' strengths also. Doing so, will allot your clients' E-business to better understand its own strengths. And please, do not forget this vital reminder: your clients' construction E-business strengths will continue to develop and redevelop, over time. Therefore, try practicing patients with each online marketing effort. Studies have shown that new online marketing strategies can take up to three years to show progress. Again, this is a study; it doesn't necessarily mean, your clients' construction E-business will encounter the same time frame to reach its goals and objectives.

Weaknesses

A. Not using the Internet effectively and efficiently as a primary promotional gateway, is a huge weakness. After all, the Internet reaches an estimated 1.4 billion people, globally. And while your clients' construction E-business may be utilizing a few online database centers to increase brand awareness, their competitors' are using the Internet to connect and make bids in foreign territories, build brand awareness, and saturate the construction industry online presence, with vital news and data about their successes and future plans. Neglecting to follow suit can be a grave weakness to your clients' E- business growth and continued success, in the online marketing environment.

B. Using inefficient Web site promotional campaigns that do not impact an increased number of Web site viewers, is another weakness. In fact, one of the biggest mistakes with online marketing, is ignoring the vast number of online information portals open to the construction industry. Even worse, is not being on the Top 250, 100, or even Top 25 Best Construction Companies list; simply because many Web site searchers use such list to determine which companies are worth investigating.

C. Not adequately outsourcing regional, national, and global competitors', is another weakness. In fact, ignoring the skill of effectively investigating competitors', can be costly in the long run. After all, with the Internet, your clients' business gains valuable insight on each one of its top 100 competitors'. Having this leverage not only increases the chances of building better brand awareness, but helps your clients' brand gain priority on these top listings and data reporting analytic charts, where competitors are being found and are using such accolades to gain bids for projects, listed around the world.

Opportunities

1. Expanding the company's brand image to additional countries, online, is the first and most important opportunity your clients' construction E-business has in its favor, when considering methods of building brand awareness, in new territories.
2. Utilizing state and/or country- Construction Associations- as information gateways and networking portals, also gives your clients' E-business an opportunity to network with industry based members who have a shared interest in the data and services your clients' E-business is offering. This is a great platform to use to offer speaking engagements about your clients' E-business, such as sharing data referencing the benefits learned about and/or knowledge gained over a certain time span, since launching the

construction E-business. Associations are built on networking and data sharing. Connecting with Construction Associations around the world, can increase your clients' construction E-business opportunities, because as their construction marketer, you will be helping your clients' learn about contracted projects, available bidding listings, and new industry related news that certainly is helpful and beneficial to your clients' overall construction E-business success.

3. Financial growth is another opportunity. After all, the more saturated the Internet becomes with your clients' company brand name, the greater the response and bid winning will be for the E-business. Monopolizing the Internet is key. Not just focusing on regional advertisements, promotions, and giveaways, but taking the company global through virtual online information data centers, defined by and for, the construction industry. Building revenue through EMarketing concepts for the construction industry, can also be a daunting task. But having a solid financial budget that enables your clients' E-business to expand its online presence and build better alliances with companies already seeking your clients' E-business services and/or products, is essential to your clients'. Connecting with others, will bring rewards that lead to financial growth. Stepping outside of the boundaries and following through, will best optimize your clients' E-business endeavors, for years to come. Just keep one thing in mind: the Internet is an endless data base of resources. And every day, more resources from around the globe are added to this information database. Therefore, your clients' company will never be absent of resources to market itself with, as long as the Internet is active. The key is: Learning how to monopolize and organize those resources. That is the power of the construction EMarketing.

4. Another opportunity, is building stronger alliances with land owners, banks, both regionally, nationally, and internationally, as well as with real estate, architectural and engineering companies. In fact, while there are countless resources available to increase a construction company's brand identity in one region and/or another part of the state or country, there are countless more resources that remain untapped around the world, by those construction companies, who refuse to take an interest in the online marketing and resource portals open to the public. But isn't this why your clients' construction E-business has an online presence in the first place?

5. Using local, national, and global events to promote the company and its brand, is another great opportunity. This could be as simple as hanging banners up at sporting events, religious organization events, concerts, school and college events and/or offering scholarships and financial aid to students currently studying to become skilled and knowledgeable in the construction industry.
6. Taking the company global and reaching new contract bids, will enable the company to continue its expansion into other parts of the world. And since China construction companies have already, seemingly, claimed South Africa, why not focus on a country that can be solely controlled by your clients' company? With more than 100 countries, surely your clients' company brand can soar beyond competitors and increase its annual

revenue earnings, in a country untapped, both online and face to face.

Threats

A. Your clients' E-business current search engine ranking on search engines, such as Google™, Yahoo™, and Bing™, can be a primary threat. After all, when a business or consumer searches for a company online, quite often that business or consumer will not search beyond the first three pages, especially when the search results total 410,000,000. Therefore, if your clients' company is not optimizing search engines around the globe, this can threaten the increased visibility and networking opportunities available to the business, especially when the company ranks 100, in a search engine query response of 100,000,000. The daunting task with this, is that, your clients' E-business must begin stepping outside the boundaries and propel into a new dimension of construction EMarketing. Utilizing 'all' search engines, globally, is the key to online search engine optimization. In fact, some E-businesses have begun implementing Web analytics through networks like Google Analytics that enables businesses to define, both the geographical and demographical regions of the world, which their daily, weekly, and monthly traffic derives from. This is great, because it enables a company to redefine its marketing efforts, without wasting money frivolously on marketing strategies that do not turn a profit. Unfortunately, not all search engines provide Web analytics. To combat this, using a template from an established Web site design agency such as Webs.com, as pointed out in previous segments, is a great way to learn about your clients' Web site's analytics, because this medium offers analytics in some of its Web site design template packages. But be aware: HTML coding, keywords, and other essential algorithms may not always be accepted in compliance with the chosen templates and/or Web site design package, you chose.

B. Offering a Web site with one domain name is certainly a threat. After all, if your clients' company's Web site listing is (www.globalconstruction.com) there are countless other construction company's using the same key words, in their domain name. So, please incorporate extended domain names. In fact, adding five or more different domain names to your clients' company Web site, through a Redirect (also referred as a Web server), will help your clients' Web site continue saturating the industries online marketplace.

C. Not researching competitors' online presence, is definitely a threat! After all, doing so helps unlock ideas for your clients' E-business- on how to better define its Web site marketing campaigns, features, and overall search engine ranking. This also enables your clients' company to understand how competitors are ranking in search engines; and learn what portals competitors are using to disseminate information about their E-business. And remember, not all competitors are using the same search engines that your clients' may be using. Take for instance, if your company registers its Web site URL in all of Japan's search engines, who will be the highest ranking U.S. construction company listed? Your clients' E-business gains control over that industries listing, in that search engine. Again, this is why optimization is key.

D. Not effectively understanding the value of online marketing concepts, is also a huge threat!

E. Lacking clarity about cyber laws not only in your state or country, but globally, is another threat. Understanding what you can and cannot do in compliance with cyber laws, helps your clients' E-business avoid unnecessary costly legalities. This is why having an EMarketer with paralegal research skills, is a plus for any construction company. It's also a plus to have a legal team to investigate such laws, because doing so gives your clients' E- business another step up over the competition.

F. Reputation management has become a key tool in helping E-businesses gain leverage over competitors online. Therefore, conducting in-depth research on your clients' company in global search engines, helps defeat enemies and clear any negative remarks and/or feedback that has been posted online about the company, which competitors can use against your clients'. To help you with this, there are service providers online that specialize in reputation management, such as (www.reputation.com), who can be instrumental in helping your clients' E-business weed out the negative online reputation that may have already begun being rooted, internationally.

TARGET MARKET

I think it's fair at this point that I confess one thing to you: The construction industry has a limited target market. However, the target market that is open to this industry, includes international mortgage companies, international land owners, international real estate agencies, globalized bankers, globalized loan managers, and globalized construction tool and equipment manufacturers. Utilizing each one of these data bases, is essential in helping construction companies build brand awareness, while establishing a professional reputation that enables the company to increase annual revenue; launch better marketing campaign promotions, and add value to the company's overall marketing presence.

In addition, introducing a construction company in a global marketplace, requires understanding each countries construction industry environment. In fact, asking questions such as: What steps are competitors using to share details about their business with networks globally and/or what strategies have competitors used to increase their ranking in industry related search engines, globally; are just as few questions that must be evaluated thoroughly, while landscaping a well-defined strategic EMarketing plan, for the construction industry. Most importantly, it's extremely valuable to understand that each competitor in the construction industry, continues unleashing its own unique online marketing strategies year after year. However, despite this fact, having an idea of how that strategy is implemented and understanding the value of your clients' competitors' Web analytics, enables your clients' construction company to soar higher than competitors and continue increasing annual revenue earnings, but on a global scale.

MARKETING OBJECTIVES

A key value underlying the American business system is reflected in the notion of a never-ending quest for improvement.[16] This is why the overall marketing objective of your clients' construction E-business must be: to share as much data and in-depth resources about the construction company, with foreign country businesses, who are constantly seeking alternatives methods to cutting cost. Furthermore, developing a strategy that offers your clients' construction E- business a precise competitive advantage and focuses on various market sectors, should also be considered. After all, marketing conditions tend to vary quite differently across the construction industry, which is broken down into various segments (residential and commercial).

Additionally, there are rate differences of growth in residential, public, retail, civil engineering, and office building sectors; making it extremely imperative to identify the niche where your clients' construction company can successfully compete. In fact, your clients' construction company's EMarketing strategy should also include focusing on attracting new account opportunities, especially for refurbishing existing properties, as well as taking on new projects.

So the marketing objective of a successful construction company operating an online presence, is to reach a global target audience, unleash the value of the company and its successes over the years, offer good valuable advice, and build better alliances with global news networks, who can better disseminate informative and valuable data about the construction E-business, but at a relatively low cost. By now, you should have a fair understanding on the value of developing an EMarketing plan. After all, many other construction marketers are absent of this data forecasting structure, which gives you an upper hand in the game of construction marketing. So don't ever relinquish your power as your clients' construction marketer, to its competitors; after all, your clients' are depending on you.

KEYWORD ANALYSIS

Keyword analysis as discussed earlier, have become quite valuable over the past few years, especially to E-business owners attempting to build and optimize an Internet presence. And with more than 500 search engines, in more than 10 countries, knowing what keywords are most often used in any given search engine, is worth investing time learning about, because your main objective in doing so, is learning how to weave your clients' URL and profile data, into as many search engines around the world as possible. This is why having a URL (Universal Resource Locator) that includes keywords assigned to your clients' Web site, is so important.

Another reason why you should consider using keywords in your clients' Web site URL, is because commonly used keywords help keyword trackers better define and/or classify keywords commonly used by search engine searchers. After all, this Internet information database helps eliminate your frustration, by providing insightful analytics on the best keywords to use for your clients' E-business, in order to be easily discovered by potential clients' and/or customers', interested in the services and/or products, your clients' construction E-business is marketing.

Take for instance, in Search Engine Colossus, (www.searchenginecolossus.com), I found a dynamic outline of search engines alphabetized by country. This list explores 317 countries and territories; and offers search engines in various languages. Therefore, it's just as important to consider using foreign terms as keywords, when deciding what keywords to use in your clients' Web site HTML code.

In fact, just recently while conducting a keyword analysis on the term-construction, I found 147,000,000 URL's at Google™.com. Now if there's 317 countries search engines listed on Search Engine Colossus, what is your best strategy to use in order to optimize your clients' construction E-business marketing performance, in order to be found by at least one-hundred search engine searchers daily? The answer: research all competitors' in every search engine, with the help of keywords that are most often analyzed by a keyword tracker. For instance, on (www.wordtracker.com), I was introduced to a compiled list of top ranking search engine terms; and also introduced to identifiable URL listings that many searchers use when looking for construction related terms. In fact, below are, both keywords and the volume of searchers using these keywords on Word Tracker®:

Keywords	**Volume**
construction	40,510
construction contractors	6,461
construction worker	4,657
construction equipment	4,287
concrete floor construction	3,937
construction jobs	3,658
bad credit construction loan	3,599
construction%20tow	3,305
construction industry	2,974
building construction	2,782

Data retrieved from http://wordtracker.com

However, when looking at another keyword identifier, such as (www.wordstream.com), I acquired an even longer populated list from a trillion keywords that best fit my keyword search. In fact, Word Stream® populated 50,000 keywords for the keyword-construction. This is the value of keyword analysis; after all, each one of your clients' construction E-business competitors' are consistently implementing new strategic EMarketing plans that help them continue ranking higher on the first and second page of countless search engines, world-wide. Therefore, lacking clarity on how to define your clients' keywords and/or what databases to begin investigating, in order to better understand your clients' competitors' online marketing platform, is in your favor. I say this because, keywords are a mere fraction of defining search engine ranking opportunities. After all, as pointed out before, search engine searchers often use *long-tail keyword phrases*. **Long-tail keyword phrases** are three to four words entered into a search engine query to define a specific populated search.

Take for instance, if you were to input the following long-tail keyword phrase in Google™: ***construction companies offering low rates***; Google™ response returns 5, 710,000 results. However, on Industrial Web Search®, the number of populated Web sites totaled 91,000,000; and on, Bing™, the total was 31,900,000. Therefore, Google™ populated the least number of search results; although, Google™ is the number one rated search engine in the U.S., U.K., Mexico, and Latin America. This is another primary reason why it's important to try using several terms to better define your search engine query.

Remember, you can also use **short-tail keyword phrases,** consisting of one, two, or three terms, such as *construction company rates*. Using short-tail keywords is not always the best alternative to conducting search engine queries. Nevertheless, despite this fact, having a list of terms that best relates to the industry and data- commonly sought in a typical search engine query by businesses, helps increase the number of populated Web site results, closely related to the particular keyword term or terms- used to locate Web sites under keywords such as- ***construction companies.***

Clearly, not only are keywords valuable to the ranking of a Web site in search engines; keywords are valuable to Web site page content and security matters, such as SSL (Security Socket Layer) Web pages. Having Security Socket Layer Web pages on your clients' Web site that requires Web site viewers to in-put intricate personal data on such forms as 'contact us', helps viewers' data remain secure and blocks intrusions. In fact, SSL Web pages are commonly used by banks, financial collection institution, academia, and all other Web sites asking Web site viewers, for sensitive data.

Meanwhile, I also must point out that each and everyday keywords will continue changing in value and search engine ranking. So, what may be useful in a search engine query in 2012, may not be a feasible list of search engine terms to use in 2015 or 2016. Therefore, staying abreast of ever changing keyword term and new definitions of keyword searches, will increase the chances of your clients' connecting with search engine seekers.

Take for instance, today, tech heads in Europe have implemented a new concept of search operation (Search Guides) that help increase the number of populated Web site responses received in any given search query. Some of the most popular Search Guides are:

- Allintitle:
- Site:
- Related:
- "Query":

Of course, using these Search Guides in front of your short-tail or long-tail keywords, not only increases the chances of locating Web site resources that best fit your particlar search, but increases the chances of you learning how to better optimize your clients' search engine registry. So instead of identifiying a populated list of search queries for the keyword term: construction, in one search engine, who calls 41,000,000; and another search enegine, which populates 7,000. Of the two, you would be more likely to locate percise databases much faster, in the search results that populated 7,000 hits; before attaining the same level of clarity in a search population of 41,000,000.

These are just a few of the intricate details I've learned over the past three years that play a key role in optimizing a construction E-business Internet presence and marketing optimization performance. Knowing how to search for key words that searchers will commonly use to define their online pathway, in order to connect with your clients' construction E-business first, is daunting. After all, your clients' E-business is competing with 80,000,000 other Web sites. But rest assure, staying aware of the seemingly endless changes currently encompassing the trend of keyword changes, will give your clients' superior levergage over competitors'. Remember, it's important to always conduct research first, before executing your EMarketing plans. After all, doing so increases your clients' online presence and better defines your clients' online business profile.

SECURITY

Implementing a structured security defense on the server and/or device hosting your clients' construction E-business Web site, is a valuable component that must be carefully studied in order to assure your clients' E-business Web site remains safe and secure; and in compliance with U.S. Department of Defense and National Cyber Security Alliances and security measures, which includes using Internet security as a professional protective measure. In fact, developing the most effective Internet security infrastructure for a medium sized office, requires having an understanding of today's innovative Internet security procedures. After all, as of 2009, according to the CIA (Central Intelligence Agency) there were 245,000,000 U.S. Internet users. [17]

And despite latest Internet security measures implemented by U.S. Department of Defense, sadly, countless E-businesses and personal computers have been hacked and sensitive data such as personal addresses, credit card data, and banking accounts, have fallen into the hands of criminals, who continue redefining the current Internet security infrastructure and unleashing vicious attacks on vulnerable Internet network systems. As a result, utilizing the most secure and stringent measures to combat unwanted intrusion must be top priority. This is why, implementing a strategic security plan, including an internal network defined with firewalls, proxy servers, and authentication list, is vital. Additionally, adding antivirus software, creating data backups, and educating employees on password protection methods, social media security and the importance of using encrypted email and doc. type files, are additional steps to enact in order to safeguard an Internet network from being viciously attacked.

Ideally, if your clients' office network is defined by an office of two to ten employees, using a WAN connection such as Point-to-Point Protocol, used between analog and digital phone lines between locations, would be a primary step towards securing the company's network. It's also important to secure all company computers with a firewall. Doing this blocks all inbound intrusions attempting to invade your hard drive and corrupt the memory database. Firewall is a software program developed to isolate potential threats and examine incoming data, in order to weed out possible intrusions that can erode a computer network security infrastructure.

In fact, Zone Alarm Pro 4.0®, with new outbound e-mail monitoring, cache cleaner, expert firewall rules, and import/export settings, is an easy interface that may be overwhelming for new users, but its defaults protect a computer's interior network from the start, and the interface is simple.[18] Adding a proxy server, is another step towards combating interior network security intrusion. Take for instance, using a proxy server such as WinGate®, will enable user management, auditing, and security features. Additionally, WinGate® proxy servers add "NNTP news, POP3, SMTP e-mail, and HTTP web browsing. [19] Adding a proxy server can "identify a Uniform Resource Locator (URL) of a server process in the request and compare that URL against filter rules previously defined to the system. In the event the URL satisfies one of the filter rules, a filter servlet associated with the satisfied filter rule, is used to filter the requested information. A filter servlet is a set of instructions that, when executed, filters the information. The filtered request is then used to retrieve information from a server process. Similarly, the same filtering process may be performed on a response from the server process destined for a client process.[20]

Next, I recommend installing an authentication list, which can be applied using Windows Server 2008® or others alike, such as Kerberos V5 Authentication®.

Adding this feature confirms the identity of any user trying to log on to a domain or access network resources.[21] And even if your using Kerberos V5 Authentication®, which is used with either a password or a smart card for interactive logon; it's imperative to be reminded of the default method of network authentication for services. For additional protection, it's also recommended, you add SSL/TLS authentication, as mentioned in the keyword segment. It is also recommended to include a passport authentication, which is a user authentication service that offers a single sign-in service.

Once you do that, it's time to install an antivirus software program, such as Trend Micro®, which offers cloud based protection that prevents daily threats, improves system performances, and stores data files in a secure package. Trend Micro® also provides privacy protection, which helps prevent identity theft, by blocking phishing emails, scan privacy settings on social media networks such as Facebook®, Pinterest®, and LinkedIn®. Plus, this software, includes a password protected manager for online accounts and a safe and secure browser for online activities such as banking and/or shopping. However, feel free to use any other top name brand Internet security software program, such as Norton®, Symantec®, or Barracuda®, which are also great privacy protectors.

After adding these components, it's time to create a database backup. Doing this enables your clients' Web master to back up only unique data. This data can include personal documents, company contracts and PDF formatted files, ledgers, invoices, acquisition forms, and financial data from the accounting department files. Furthermore, using a backup system enables your clients' Web master, to conduct a daily and weekly back-up schedule that will be helpful in maintaining control over the flow of data shared between employees who are sharing the company network. Backing up data is good because it enables the Web master to save data to an extended hard-drive; instead of saving data on an employee's hard-drive on their laptop.

However, I do recommend saving additional copies of data on different extended hard drives or flash drives. In fact, you can use a zip file embedded in additional zip files. This will create your first layer of protection. From there, you can add as many layers of protection on that zip file as you'd like. Simply keep clicking the compressing file on every file created, until you feel comfortable with the number of security layers added to that file.

You can also save data on a removable flash drive that easily inserts in a USB port. These devices are great components to have, because of the amount of storage space they allot. For instance, Scan Disk® offers a flash drive with 32 GB and 64 GB. Toshiba® offers an extended hard drive that has 500 GB. Using these methods enables each employee to define a safe and memorable way of securing their passwords and sensitive data. In fact, using a long-tail phrase such as 'ConnyPennFosterCollege' is a great way to begin disguising each individual employee's personal log-in data, and prevent someone from accessing that employee's information. Therefore, I suggest having employees define passwords and/or usernames, with upper and lower case letters, symbols, and numbers, such as: Ashford1uNiversitY#. This certainly is a great way to defeat criminals!

Again, using SSL certificates and configuring the email program through the settings menu on a device, and clicking the option to activate the encryption- is key to configuring the security of your clients' computer network. Furthermore, if your clients' construction E-business, Web master uses an Exchange email account, find a designated area for security settings that can be clearly identified whether encryption/security is enabled for the incoming and outgoing connections and for, your clients' E-business employee's Exchange accounts. In the event this isn't so, check with the email provider to see whether the provider supports encryption, and consider switching to a service that allows SSL/TLS encryption.[22]

And since employees must utilize social media to increase marketing communication with leads and clients', educating employees about social media security measures, is another step that must be implemented. Take for instance, Microsoft® offers 11 steps to implement in order to secure social media safety. Some of those secure media safety tips, include: using caution when clicking links embedded within post and/or promotional marketing campaigns on Facebook® and Twitter®. This means: avoid using personal data in online profiles such as names of family members, pets, birthdates, and other identifiable data that can be used to compile an image profile on you and/or your clients'.

Another step to remember, is to not trust email from strangers. This means, DO NOT OPEN EMAILS THAT YOU ARE UNFAMILIAR WITH! After all, there are email pranksters using names of people with profiles on Facebook® and other social media Web pages, you post data in, to develop profile records of people's history.

Doing so enables them to gain credit in your name, open accounts in foreign banking systems and/or do even worse damage, purchase life insurance claims. Therefore, always alarm employees to ignore ALL incoming emails and/or links layered in emails on social media; no matter who those emails are from. To be wise, encourage employees to compile a list of those they often get emails from and store that data in their email account files. Place stars on each account. So that emails from duplicated sources attempting to utilize email addresses already stored in this data base, cannot allot accessibility to those sensitive files and/or be a source of accessibility.

Next, please alert all employees to not allow social media networks' to scan your clients' e-mail address list. After all, the Web site might use this information to send email messages to everyone in your clients' contact list or even everyone you've ever sent an email message to, with that email address.[23] In fact, Microsoft® shared a brief note in a recent interview conveying how important it is to determine if the company has a policy about visiting certain Web sites on the company network; after all, an employee should never reveal data about their job title, location, and additional details that can aid criminals in building profile sheets on vulnerable social media members.

Also, it's essential that employees understand the value of using privacy browsing, particularly when using Internet Explorer. By clicking the tools icon with ridged edges, next to the star icon, in the upper right hand corner of the Internet Explorer task bar, the employee should scroll down to the 'Safety' link and click In Private Browsing. Doing this, disenables outside viewers from storing data as the history of Web pages viewed by the user account, cache, and cookies. Next, disenable all pop-up blockers through the configuring settings on the device; this will prohibit ads and unwanted Web pages from popping up when surfing the Internet. I also recommend blocking external content and avoid viewing unidentifiable attachments that can host Trojans™ and/or viruses.

Just keep in mind, work place security is much different than personal computer security; therefore, it's important to define stringent policies. Generally, the policy isn't one large document, but rather a series of specific documents that each address one procedure or asset. One of the tougher aspects of developing a security policy, is finding a balance between trust and control. Enterprises must decide on the trust model they want to have—trusting everyone all the time, trusting no one at any time, or trusting some people some of the time—while deciding how much control any one employee should have over delicate procedures and operations. Making policies too restrictive or difficult to follow, will lead to employees ignoring them, while the idea of 'too-lax' policies, can lead to trouble and poor attitudes. The goal of a security policy, is to find a reasonable consensus that allows protection of assets, while keeping all affected parties involved and effective.[24]

Clearly, as you can see these are some of the steps I recommend implementing in order to combat network intrusion, hacking, email phishing, and identity theft, within the interior network of a medium sized company, operating with a minimum of two to ten employees. Of course, while this list seems quite detailed, there are countless additional measures, you should also consider as precautionary steps towards maintaining control over the security of your clients' construction E-business Web site. Therefore, hiring a professionally trained and academia accredited Internet Security personnel, is vital to your clients' E-business online security infrastructure.

COMPETITORS

Like all industries in the marketplace there will always be competitors in the construction E-business industry, who will have better defined EMarketing strategies, are more knowledgeable and skilled technicians on everything from Web site development, EMarketing laws, to having basic Internet security operations and procedure skills. Due to this, and as mentioned before, it's imperative to thoroughly conduct research on your competitors', especially if your clients' construction company continues to rank on the tenth, twentieth and/or one-hundredth page of a populated search engine query. After all, if your clients' construction company isn't populating on the first three pages of any search engine query, chances of being found by consumers, contract bidders, project offers and/or associations or news media resources interested in services offered by your client, that perhaps can provide a spearheading advertising article to draw viewers to your clients' Web site, is slim to none.

In fact, chances are, your clients' construction E-Business isn't optimizing its online presence and/or utilizing the Internet to better structure its overall visual display. Even worse, if your clients' construction E-Business is not listed on the Top 250 list populated by the Engineering News Record®, whose list of contractors is shared with readers internationally. Or, on the list of the world's top construction companies defined by Ranker.com, [25] who compiles its list, based upon the revenue earned yearly by construction companies; then it's time to rethink your clients' online marketing strategies'. This is another reason why defining an EMarketing plan structured with strategic metrics compiled from thorough investigated research is important. But have no fear, there are additional steps you can implemented to better position your clients' ranking on search engines that will help them out rank their competitors' time and again. Take the following steps below for instance:

Step I

a. *Investigate what search engines your clients' competitors' are registered with, both nationally and internationally. Doing this gives you some idea of what your clients' competitors' are doing to spread the word about their services, products, and data about their company.*

b. *Investigate what news articles have been written over the past three to five years about your clients' competitors'. Finding this essential data, gives you an opening to approach those news worthy mediums as gateways of sharing stories about your clients' products, services and/or Web site.*

c. *Find out if your clients' competitors' have received any awards or honorable mentions in the past three to five years. If so, apply for those same awards and honorable mentions. If you learn that those awards increased the value of your clients' competitors' E-business, why not take the same step towards building a respectable brand name for your client?*

d. *What associations are your clients' competitors' using to optimize their Web site presence? Connecting with associations is a great way to build a company brand name and make better connections that increase business growth and development. Being a part of an association enables a business to build a line of communication with members and business partners, regionally, nationally, and internationally. Associations also are great for supporting company innovativeness. Therefore, do not neglect to become familiar with online industry related associations.*

e. *What amount of page content management are competitors' using to increase their Web site search engine ranking? As pointed out before, merely registering your clients' Web site URL with search engines, isn't enough to attract attention and spearhead a loyal flow of interested businesses, seeking to build alliance with your clients' E-business.*

Step II

a. *Increase awareness and interest in your clients' company and what the company has to offer, by building stronger online alliances with businesses who have global offices. Using the Internet as a database should be your first and only primary resource for implementing new leads and measuring your clients' E-business success.*

b. *Be authentic with your advertising methods, especially those implemented for online marketing campaigns. Traditional approaches to offline marketing are still usable online. However, online marketing strategies require more time and effort to establish. Again, this is why developing an EMarketing plan is key. Not only does having an EMarketing plan eliminate wasting time researching dead end leads. Instead, having an EMarketing plan increases your ability to beat competitors'. After all, EMarketing plans help you forecast how to approach various mediums of communication online, to increase awareness about your clients' services and/or products.*

c. *Always be willing to educate Web site viewers through online digital multimedia, in any one of your clients' Web site Web pages. This can involve having clients' give a speaking engagement that can be accessed via Webinars and online conferences. Studies conducted and shared through the pages of Internet Retailer®, conveyed that many Japanese and Chinese business men, are now interested in building business alliances using these new mediums of communication.*

Step III

a. *Persuasion: what is your clients' Web site offering to persuade viewers' to connect and seek additional information and/or follow through to make a business proposal? Reconsidering how to approach Web site viewers should be another priority. Neglecting to keep this focus positions your clients' E-business below competitors'; in many instances, because competitors' are investing top dollar- trying to out beat your clients'. Therefore, take time to sketch your thoughts on persuasive components that can be incorporated in your clients' online marketing infrastructure.*

b. *All online ad banners should be authentic in terminology and enveloped in important details about the company and its mission. Don't neglect to optimize ad banners, with essential data about the company. Using left and right side ad banners that scale a Web site's columns, enhances advertising methods.*

c. *Web site page content should be original, often updated, and offer educational clarity on various industry related issues. This is a great way to positon clients' E-businesses as an expert in the field. Offer certificate based educational learning experiences, with the use of today's free educational course rooms, provided by superior educational institutions, such as Harvard Business School, Oxford Business School, Taft University, and Cornell University. In fact, you can find many great college level courses for free using (www.alison.com). This, Ireland secret knowledge base informed Web site, is a treasure filled with endless data on every industry related subject, from how to define HTML coding, to marketing on social media Web sites.*

Step VI

a. *Focus on building a prospective clientele, globally. Through the use of the Internet, you can research companies in other countries that may be able to build bridges with your clients'. Therefore, never neglect to research global construction database.*

b. *Redefine your clients' E-business mission, goals, and objectives, in correlation with competitors'. If your clients' mission statement and focus has changed over the years, since establishing itself, it's time to revise it and incorporate additional ideas for the company mission. This is a great way to identify new goals for your client's marketing strategies.*

Step V

a. *Implement worthy news on various industry related issues on your clients' Web site. This helps increase dialogue with Web site viewers, who can post remarks about industry related news on your clients' Web site Web page designated for forum feedback. Most often, E-businesses use blogs to do this, which is another tool mentioned previously. But using search engine news resources such as Search Engine Watch and/or Search Engine Land, are great resources to use in order to find industry related news that best fits your clients' overall marketing objectives-build brand awareness.*

As you can see from the steps listed, having an understanding of competitors' online advertising methods, knowing what database resources to investigate, and how to eliminate using ideas that can stagnate marketing performances, will enable your clients' E-business to continue soaring ahead of the line and find better leads that connect to revenue earning business alliances. More importantly, having a step or two up on your clients' competition, will always enable your clients' E-business to better position itself and receive a better response rate to ads disseminated via the Internet. But all of this cannot be achieved if you as a construction marketer doesn't take the time to implement some, if not all of these well-researched strategies shared with you in the pages of this EMarketing plan.

"*Fear never accomplishes anything, so be bold and soar*"-

Dr. V. Polite

Actions:

Implementing a contingency plan is also important because it gives you the opportunity to analyze difficulties and risk associated with your clients' E-business. In fact, you should:

- Challenge generating exposure that drives consumers to the E-business Web site
- Be aggressive enough to combat the marketing efforts of all of your clients' competitors'
- Never be afraid to establish an online presence that cannot compete because a competitor is already saturating the industry information gateway with details about its services and products
- Always understand that your clients' E-business cannot sustain successfully, without a committed effort from you as the primary EMarketer

- Never be afraid to push your client to pour additional finance into their online and offline marketing strategies

Objectives:

The main objective, is gaining customer confidence in your clients' products and/or services, by using Web site visual display and multimedia as the primary approach to conducting business. One way to achieve this objective, is determining your clients' E-business strengths in comparison with competitors'; this was mentioned in previous segments. Another way to achieve this objective, is taking advantage of all opportunities afforded to your clients' E-business and its online visual display. Combating all threats, as mentioned before, is valuable to your clients' E-business reputation management, which should always remain top priority, especially when there are prospective clients' always seeking professionally, skilled, and well-trained construction companies that get the job done, while avoiding violating state, city, or federal regulations and business practices.

Market Trends

Internet consumers are savvier about their purchasing power in various ways; take for instance:

- They're more likely to invest time reading and researching what a Web site is professing; this is a good reason why, you should also focus more attention on good Web site page content management

- They're less likely to concern themselves with the appearance of sales letters sent via direct-mail. Instead, they're more likely to be drawn to savvier marketing approaches that outwit other construction E-businesses, using identical methods

While these are just a few market trends, it's highly recommended, you always seek out new market trends. I cannot stress this enough. Lacking an interest in staying up to date with market trends, will impact your clients' over all online performance. Most importantly, try to have fun learning all of the data you can about the industry, but do not neglect to investigate what construction companies are doing in other countries. That means, find out what other construction companies are doing in Japan, China, Africa, and Mexico.

MARKET GROWTH

Along with the steps already mentioned in previous segments of this EMarketing plan, focusing on market growth, is also key for understanding how to increase a clients' business opportunities. In fact, building a new market growth strategy that will render unlimited revenue earnings for your client should also include:

- Remembering it's important to understand the online construction marketing platform and how often it changes from year to year. What was best in marketing last year, is not always best for this year

- Also remember to develop a strategic EMarketing plan that proves effective and beneficial for your clients' E-business and its long-term growth opportunities

Forecasting and revising EMarketing plans should be done weekly, monthly, and yearly. After all, an EMarketing plan, is the blue print to understanding how to find treasures buried deeply within the endless number of Web pages registered online. Furthermore, as a construction EMarketer, having a hold on how to optimize the data available online, gives you leverage many other construction marketers lack. Certainly, anyone with a sincere drive to succeed in online marketing for the construction industry, shouldn't mind investing time gathering necessary data, such as this I've provided; and building upon this platform. Merely because, such valuable data unleashes your confusion about competiting and winning more contracts and earning more revenue for your clients'.

TECHNICAL MATTERS

Considering today's E-commerce environment is so competitive, having a firm grip on technical matters affecting your clients' E-business, is another intricate component, you cannot ignore. After all, technical matters involve: Web site search ability, multimedia, auto-responders, feedback forms, Web site hosting and publishing, and monthly Web site maintenance; this can be anything from maintaining security updates, Microsoft® software updates, page content management, adding additional data to the Web site and/or removing old data that's irrelevant and/or that has been posted on the Web site for some time, but not organized. So to help you better understand these technical matters, below is an outline of a few additional steps I strongly believe, will not only increase your clients' Web site viewer response, but enable your clients' E-business to continue redefining its focus and mastering its position in cyberspace marketability.

Just remember: When one door shuts in your face, there are one-million more you haven't discovered, tucked away within those countless Internet resources, populated in search engine queries.

Now let's talk about *web search ability.* Interestingly, according to a study conducted by Yale University, Internet search engines such as Yahoo™, Bing™, and others alike, including Yale's local Google Search Appliance, which uses an automated system that helps searchers find and follow Web links and analyze and index Web page content, for search relevancy, should be considered. Ideally, such automated search systems are collectively classified as: Web crawlers or Web spiders. This classification emphasis links and pages, which are crucial to understanding how Web search engines work; after all, crawlers can only find your clients' Web pages if they have links to help find those pages, because search engines do not rank whole Web sites. Instead, Web sites are ranked by popularity and page content relevancy, based on each individual Web page within a Web site. Therefore, each page of your clients' Web site needs to be optimized for better search engine request, and perfectly-linked to other Web pages within your clients' Web site, because from a search engine's point of view, each Web page stands alone.[26]

Take for instance, using the URL (www.constructionindustryprofession.com) as a primary Web site address, is not enough to impact your clients'

Web site's finder search ability. In fact, in order for this URL to become a key Web crawler, a construction EMarketer would need to register every Web page in a clients' Web site, with every single search engine in the world. So if your clients' Web site consists of 1 or more pages, every Web page must be registered, individually. Therefore, the "about us" Web page, "services" Web page, "contact us" Web page, and all other Web pages, must be registered with not just the four or five search engines you're already aware of. But 'all' search engines around the globe. Optimizing this medium of registration entry not only enables your clients' E-business to build a favorable search engine registry reputation, but it increases your clients' E-business search engine ranking.

The next technical matter is *multimedia.* This intricate component is important because it wasn't until the mid-90s when multimedia was integrated into Web sites as a method of increasing viewer experience. And since multimedia has become common place, multimedia mediums such as YouTube®, Daily motion©, Vimeo®, Metacafe®, Flickr®, Internet Archive®, Live Leak®, and 4shared®, are now some of the best alternative mediums to upload digital media and .jpg images, your clients' may seek to share with others, hoping to gain additional leverage over the competition.

Besides, not only is your clients' E-business providing Web site viewers a visual display of the services, products, or goods offered, but your clients' can utilize multimedia to drive potential client interest; and possibly, close many contract deals- all via the Internet. Disseminating Web site multimedia through various platforms, such as press releases, email distribution, and registered multimedia networks, is a valuable asset to invest in; not once a year, but monthly. In fact, according to Ginger Multimedia, using videos can help improve your search engine ranking as well. [27]

Plus, multimedia can also:

- enhance your clients' Web site visual landscape
- attract affiliate marketing links
- increase Web site traffic
- help sell products or services easier and less expensively
- cuts cost

By adding multimedia, your clients' Web site is 53 times more likely to appear on the first page of a Google search. The most popular search engine used around the globe.

Furthermore, if your clients' Web site offers informative page content that's useful and inspiring to another E-business closely related to your client's industry, quite often, such E-businesses seeking to gain leverage over other E-businesses, will query your clients' E-business with interest of linking their Web site to your clients', which will help that E-business increase additional Web traffic, not only for their Web site, but your clients' as well. This is why adding multimedia is so great for your clients' Search Engine Optimization (SEO), especially if your clients' are seeking to be found in countless search engines internationally.

Now let's concentrate on the value of adding *auto-responders*. After all, auto-responders are integrated in the Web site's HTML code, to allow immediate responses to emails sent to your clients' E- business. Adding an auto-responder to the Web site's 'contact us' page, assures Web site viewers their request for additional data and/or details about the company are being investigated with superior professional interest. Not only does this position your clients' E-business with a new platform for on-going communication, but it conveys the level of professionalism the company strives on; and exposes a little about its ethics towards business correspondence. In fact, in an article shared on (www.Small Business Advocate.com), I learned that providing well-written auto-responder messages in emails, is a great way to build trust with potential customers'. It is further suggested that E-business owners draft a signature file that includes prewritten messages to be embedded within the frame of an outgoing email.

For example, if you're anticipating being away from your desk and/or office for a period of time, sending a courteous auto-responder email message, is key to sustaining the on-going development of communication, with whomever you're disseminating such communication to and/or with. Ideally, a great way of writing such a message would be: *Thank you for contacting me; however, I'm away from my office from 10/30/2014-11/4/2014.*

Furthermore, auto-responders can be saved in a signature file stored on your clients' hard drive, an extended hard drive or other devices your clients' use to save important data. Having this data stored collectively and well organized, helps clients' save time when they need to quickly access the saved data and use it. In fact, it's best to outline several different auto-responder messages, so at any given time, such messages can be integrated in Web site email responses, without delay in reaching its rightful recipient.

Additionally, feedback forms are the next most valuable asset to provide Web site viewers. By simply integrating feedback forms within a Web page, viewers can share comments, ask questions, and share additional details about their query. Your clients' can also use these mediums of communication as gateways to building better email marketing lists, network and/or share data about the business. Although, one way to gain access to email listings, would be through Equifax®, Tele check®, or any other credit bureau. Just simply sign on to the Web site and navigate your way through the tabs that leads to the Web page offering leads to email addresses. You can actually attain email listing based upon geographic and demographics.

Meanwhile, having a clear understanding on how to combat technical matters, is essential to your clients' E-business. This is why as a construction marketer, it is your responsibility to render the best professionalism and well researched data to clients'. Doing so not only increases your value to that client, but increases your value as a construction marketer.

MOOD BOARDS

Mood boards are inspirational boards, primarily used in a variety of art expressions to convey ideas about a specific design. In fact, a mood board can be useful to establish the aesthetic feeling of a Web site. And quite often are integrated into the process somewhere after wireframes and before Web site design mockups are begun.

Ideally, some of the things explored in mood boards are: photography style, color palettes, typography, and page content format patterns. Perhaps your client likes soft colors or gritty and tuff textures. Developing mood boards help convey a collage of colors, various textures, and high resolution glossy images that evoke a specific style or feeling in a Web site design platform.

In addition, mood boards are meant to be casual; after all, mood boards enable a Web site developer to share design ideas for the Web site and extend the opportunity for the Web developer to acquire feedback from a client, before pouring too much time in one assignment; only to discover, the client doesn't like the Web site design idea being presented. A good example for mood board presentations, is offering your client a color palette with various shades of strong masculine hues. This can include: blacks, browns, navy, different blues and greys; tangerine, mandarin, and of course, shades of wood grain or even, steel. Offering a client this opportunity enables the client to play a role in electing the right color scheme for their Web site.

In fact, I've researched the number of construction marketers applying traditional color schemes to Web sites, such as: orange trimmed with various grey hues; browns accented with beige borders, and red font. I've even seen different contrasting colors of blues: light, navy, sky, ocean, and baby blue. However, when examining one construction company's Web site and comparing it to another, what makes each Web site stand alone, is what evokes the Web site searcher to elect the Web site best suited to their visual appeal. For instance, you can show clients' color palettes on Google™ at (www.Google.com/images/color_palettes). This will give you a general understanding of various colors. Or, you can use a hexadecimal color chart, which will give you a different scale of colors to choose from.

Next, adding vibrant, high resolution images that convey the specific elements, you seek to share in your clients' Web page presentation, is another component to consider. After all, using construction images of equipment, construction workers on the job, projects built, and other images closely related to the industry, helps impact viewers' interest and response to the page content on your clients' Web site. Be sure that when adding images to your clients' Web site Web pages, to use the device settings to format each image before adding the image to the Web page. This is recommended, because if images are not measured correctly using the settings format, those images will cause your clients' Web site Web pages to upload very slowly. Also, please be sure to save images that you compile from the Internet, to a file within the Web site file you've created for the actual Web site. Once you determine what images best fits your clients' Web page design, it's time to consider adding different typographies.

Typography, is the art and technique of arranging various font types to be used in marketing ads, in order to attract the attention of viewers. Ideally, typography is performed by typesetters, compositors, typographers, graphic designers, art directors, manga artists, comic book artists, graffiti artists, clerical workers, and everyone else in the business of arranging typography for a product and/or service provider. After all, the use of typography has a long time history. In fact, marketers' have used typography to convey promotional print and online advertising material for clients', over the years, in many formats.

In addition, it's also important to consider sharing a few textures, with your client to see if he or she would be interested in adding such textures to their Web pages. A great place to find textures, is also through Google™. In fact, you can search for textures such as steel, various wood grains, brick, cement, and simulated woods; using these textures will give your clients' Web site, a distinguished appeal that sets their Web site apart from competitors'. This is what makes using textures in Web page Web site designs so valuable. After all, when you as a construction marketer view your clients' competitors' Web sites, what is it that you're drawn to on that particular Web site?

This is why, I suggest creating sample mood boards as often as possible; and apply the techniques shared in this section, to begin developing dynamic mood boards for clients' as a method of assuring them, you are knowledgeable and skillful about the ideas you seek to implement as a professional construction marketer. To learn more about developing mood boards, log on to (www.sampleboard.com).

WEBSITE PRESENTATIONS

When I initially began studying Web site development, I was introduced to a Web site that immediately grabbed my attention: Web sites That Suck.com (www.webpagesthatsuck.com). This Web site was designed with the idea of demoting and ridiculing Web site developers who provide clients' with trashy Web site designs. On this Web site, I was also introduced to some interesting data many Web site developers lack clarity on. So in an attempt to encourage better Web site development for construction EMarketing, I've compiled some data that will help construction marketers' achieve optimal visual display success, with professionally designed Web site Web pages. Doing so will not only enlighten you about the differences in Web site developments, but also share details to consider implementing, when designing and/or redesigning a Web site for a client, in the construction industry.

Today there are two primary styles of Web sites: *static* and *dynamic*. The difference between the two, is that, static Web sites are designed for personal use and/or small businesses. These Web sites are simple to design and can be easily hosted. However, the disadvantage of using a static Web site design, is that static Web site development requires expertise to update Web pages regularly, which can be costly if you lack HTML and/or XHTML coding experience. Furthermore, another disadvantage of using static Web sites, is this style of Web site is not easily navigational for the Web site viewer and/or the page content may get stagnate.

On the other hand, dynamic Web sites differ, because these Web sites require more functional applications, such as components integrated for E-commerce; and works as a system that staff and users can relate to. However, much like static Web sites, dynamic Web sites also have disadvantages. First of all, dynamic Web sites are expensive to develop and require an extensive timeframe to complete as well as maintain; due to the continued need to update each Web page's content. Plus, dynamic Web sites cost a lot more to host.

This is why in many instances, small business and personal Web sites, are developed in static format. Of course, I do encourage construction marketing Web site developers to stick with the style of Web site design that best works for you and the client. After all, doing so cuts the design time in half and eliminates unnecessary frustration.

However, if using dynamic Web site Web pages, is what your client seeks, I recommend defining a Web site approach that best meets your expertise. And if your client still wants bells and whistles, be sure to provide the client with an estimated cost of the overall project development. This can be achieved by calculating the number of hours it takes to develop a Web site that is secure and non-hackable, with the use of HTML coding specified by, for example <meta description= " construction" />. There is one way to get around this issue, and that's using Adobe Dreamweaver™ or Joomla™, as your Web site developer and editor. Using one of these software apps is great, because it also enables you to host the Web site and add as many domain names to this Web site. If that isn't enough, you can also research the best alternative methods to developing dynamic Web sites; on (www.developer.dynamicweb.com). This Web site is great for tutorials and connecting you with other Web site developers, who have experience with dynamic Web site Web page development. This network of developers offers a forum to share questions and/or find additional resources from forum registered users, who may have tips to offer. Also provided, is documentation, which is useful in explaining Dynamic Web installation, navigation searches, and log-in functionality.

Okay, now that you have clarity on the two types of Web site designs, let's evaluate how a professional Web site should be built. Using a two column Web site design approach, enables the designer to maintain a strict anchor guide on both sides of the Web page. Although this can be challenging to combat when working with three column Web sites, because you lack the space for various widgets to be integrated in the Web page, in the first place. Moreover, in an 800×600 pixel screen, there is a limited amount of real estate on screen. The content is more important, and so, if the small 2 column design is what is needed to prevent the content from being cramped then 2 columns it is. [28]

However, in some instances, using a three column Web site page design may be best for your clients' presentation. After all, the page content is better centered, post are shorter, and displays are less cluttered. This is great because it enables a Web site developer to balance the Web page design professionally. Footers are required because they not only balance the Web page design, but they enable Web page users to better navigate back up to the top of the Web page and/or click through to additional

Web pages in the Web site, without going back to the top of the index.html page. Typically, a professional Web site footer often mimics the header, with the same hyperlinks, such as: home, about, services, and contact pages. You also will find the copyright date, social media icon buttons, and additional links and data about the Web site owner and/or Web master, located in the footer.

The next dimension of developing a professional Web site, is the election of the number of Web pages needed to convey enough evoking data about the company and services being offered. Offering Web site viewers engaging content as mentioned time and again, both through Web page imagery and capturing dialogue that evokes interest in what is being shared and/or offered, is what a Web site developer and EMarketer must know how to do. After all, the Web site viewer, is the primary judge of a Web site's long-term success. And considering the fact that most Web site viewers are forced to comb through extensive populated Web site Web pages during a search; offering Web pages that grab the attention of Web site viewers immediately, is essential. Therefore, learning how to design a Web site that pleases Web site viewers within seconds of the viewer arriving on the index.html Web page, is a part of the construction EMarketer's, fiduciary duty.

Another intricate component to developing great professional Web site Web pages, is building confidence in your Web site viewer, immediately after he or she arrives at the Web site. Trust me: this is not easily done. So be sure to utilize all Web pages within the Web site effectively, to woo the Web site viewer to scroll through each Web page in the Web site. That means, not all digital multimedia should be viewed on the index.html homepage. Making use of digital multimedia to convey data about the history of the company and/or services being offered, can be the best step towards gaining that Web site viewer's attention.

Meanwhile, to really stand out from the competition, perhaps integrating a talking head spokesperson on your clients' Web pages, will attract, both large and small clients. After all, a talking head spokesperson delivers a fierce visual display of a real live person walking back and forth across the screen of the Web page. These plug-ins are easily embedded within a Web site's HTML code and can be positioned anywhere on a Web page.

In fact, over the years, talking heads have gained a great deal of attention from Web site developers, who implement these animations as mediums of attraction and professional spokespersons for E-businesses. Generally, the fee for a talking head's HTML code ranges from $250.00 or more, for 30-60 words. Some talking head spokespersons can even cost $500.00, for 60-80 words. To find the best alternative, try conducting a search in three different search engines, and determine which company offers the best price. After all, using a speech agent, is a great asset to provide for your clients' Web site presence.

Clearly as stated before, keywords are another great asset to consider when developing Web page content. Therefore, be sure to use the keyword tracker, mentioned before. After all, using this component will not only cut your time span in half trying to think of keywords. Instead, it will enable you to optimize your creative writing skills differently than other Web site developers and construction marketers. Just remember, the first thing a Web site viewer sees when landing on your clients' Web page, is the visual displays embedded into each Web page.

The next general focus should be- page content. After all, this element conveys the essential data being delivered on a clients' E-business Web site, to evoke viewer interest, gain feedback, and possibly close a business deal. And sadly, if your clients' Web site design and Web site Web page content does not capture the Web site viewer's response immediately, there is a great chance of losing that Web site viewer for good.

EMARKETING LAWS

Although Web site presentations and page content are important factors in any Web site E-business development, as a construction marketer, it is essential to understand, both national and international EMarketing laws. After all, the Federal Trade Commission enacted online advertising and marketing laws in 2000, hoping to curve erroneous online marketing campaigns. Since doing so, additional EMarketing laws have been plugged and gained a substantial amount of attention in the media; not only in America, but globally. In fact, Canada's new EMarketing law enacted in 2014, places a strenuous burden on EMarketers', hoping to lure online consumers' living in Canada, with enticing Web site designs and exceptional products offered at reduced cost. This is because new laws now prohibit online marketers' from sending unsolicited marketing email messages to Canadian residence, without prior written consent.

However, unfortunately, not all EMarketers are aware of this new law and/ or any other EMarketing laws already in existence. After all, today, many EMarketers possess certification and no degree in the EMarketing industry. Learning this evoked me to sincerely invest time completing a degree, not only in EMarketing, but Computer Maintenance Technology, with a certification diploma in Web site development, and paralegal studies. In fact, if you're interested in completing a degree in EMarketing, I highly recommend Ashford University Forbes School of Business®. The tuition is economical and the course outlines beat out any other course outline for EMarketing studies, I've investigated over the past three years. I also recommend completing the Chris Farrell Social Media Marketing diploma program offered on (www.Alison.com). After all, it's without cost.

Furthermore, as a construction marketer, it's also valuable to understand both intellectual property and civil and criminal law procedures. In fact, I've learned the importance of staying abreast of international EMarketing laws. After all, I, like many other EMarketers, prefer to provide clients' with superior, updated, essential EMarketing knowledge that enables them to remain one step ahead of their competition. As a result, I've compiled a few EMarketing laws, which I believe should be recognized by professional construction marketers', who pride themselves on offering construction EMarketing services.

Ideally, one of the most important informational resources offered by the Federal Trade Commission, is the Advertising and Marketing Internet Law guide, they've prepared for marketers' and E-commerce business owners'. Although this guide was developed in 2000, many of these laws and procedures remain in place, still today. Therefore, take a few moments and review these new and old laws enacted around the globe by various countries, hoping to instill a sense of security in the minds of their citizens, who are more dependent on the Internet to attain services, products, and business networking with other companies around the globe.

And although, the Federal Trade Commission is a primary law enforcer for Internet advertising and marketing, the FCC (Federal Communications Commission) and the WTO (World Trade Organization), both stand firm behind the implementation of Internet marketing laws, ordinances, rules, and regulations. So researching EMarketing laws should become a second nature for all construction marketers'; simply because, our clients' depend on us to provide them with valuable, reliable, up to date resources that enable them to compete with competitors' in the online marketplace environment.

In fact, to me, the first essential EMarketing law that should be adhered to, is affixing a copy right date and ownership recognition on the footer of all Web site Web pages. The signature copyright should look like this: *2015© Construction EMarketing. All rights reserved.* If the Web master who develops the Web site, used images from resources other than his/her own, acknowledgement should also be included, such as: *2015© Construction EMarketing. All rights reserved. All posted images used on this Web site are from www.google.com/images. Permission to use these images is not required.*

Certainly, this is a sure way to protect your clients' E-business from being served with a complaint about the use of .jpg., .png and/or bitmap images that may have been stolen from some other online source and used on their clients' Web site, without their knowledge. Surely, there are many other online resources that enable Web site developers and/or those seeking images for various reasons, to be used for non-commercial purposes, such as Bing™ and Yahoo!™ Although these are primary resource used globally by Web site developers and others', who often neglect to research rather these images can be used for commercial use; as an informed and knowledgeable construction marketer, it is in your best interest to always investigate rather images used for clients' Web site Web pages, are free of copyright protection.

In fact, in many instances, it's best to locate images from sources outside the U.S., which often are not copyright protected by U.S. citizens. After all, you don't want to use graphic art designs being used by others, who can file a civil complaint against your client, for copyright infringement. This can cause some serious problems. Such as that which I pointed out earlier, in the search engine segment.

Meanwhile, another critical EMarketing law that should be adhered to, is honest page content. Using honest page content is important because deceptive page content can be held liable. And in many instances, such liabilities infringe upon the success of any E-business. Take for instance, the Federal Trade Commission Act, Section 5 explains deceptive page content as misleading and encouraging consumers' to make purchases on products and/or services that aren't legitimate.

Furthermore, the FTCA, explains this law by expressing that "advertising must tell the truth and not mislead consumers. A claim can be misleading if relevant information is left out or if the claim implies something that's not true. For example, a lease advertisement for an automobile that promotes, $0 down, may be misleading if significant and undisclosed charges are due at lease signing. [29]

And because such laws exist, EMarketers' and Web site developers are being held accountable for not investigating these laws; even though, clients' may confess that all data on their Web site, is accurate and true. Therefore, in order to protect yourself from being held liable and responsible for such, make sure the Web site you are conducting EMarketing for has a disclaimer, which is certainly the cheaper alternative to hiring legal representation to defend your client from a disgruntled consumer. Currently, there are many Web site disclaimers, however, I found a few samples online I'd like to share with you.

The first disclaimer sample I located, was found on the U.S. Department of the Interior Web site. This disclaimer is a great example for any Web site developer and/or EMarketer, to consider using on a clients' Web site, because the U.S. Department of the Interior extends the fair use act so others can mimic their disclaimers:

"Copyright:

Generally, materials produced by federal agencies are in the public domain and may be reproduced without permission. However, not all materials appearing on this Web site are in the public domain. Some materials have been donated or obtained from individuals or organizations and may be subject to restrictions on use.

You may consult our staff for details on specific items. We are aware of use restrictions applicable to some items or collections, but we cannot confirm copyright status for any item. We recommend that you contact the United States Copyright Office at The Library of Congress to search currently copyrighted materials.

Please note that because we cannot guarantee the status of specific items, you use materials found in our holdings at your own risk. Images on our Web site (or a third party site where we share images, such as Flickr) which are in the public domain may be used without permission. However, you should investigate whether this image is, in fact, in the public domain because we cannot warrant or guarantee the legal status of these images. If you use images from our site or collections, we ask that you credit us as the source. Please note that some images on our site have been obtained from other organizations. Permission to use these images should be obtained directly from those organizations" (www.doi.gov).[30]

"Trademarks:

Many of the trademarks, service marks, trade dress and logos (collectively, the "Trademarks") displayed on the Web site, including the Department of the Interior and its Bureaus are registered and/or unregistered common law trademarks of the Department of the Interior and/or its Bureaus. The trademarks of third parties may also be displayed on this Web site. Nothing contained on this Web site should be construed as granting, by implication or otherwise, any license or right to use any Trademarks displayed on the Web site without the express written permission of the Department of the Interior or any third party that may own the Trademarks displayed on the site. Any unauthorized use of the Trademarks or any other images or content on this Web site, except as authorized in these Terms and Conditions, is strictly prohibited"(www.doi.gov).

"Restriction of Liability:

Company name makes no claims, promises or guarantees about the accuracy, completeness, or adequacy of the contents of this Web site and expressly disclaims liability for errors and omissions in the contents of this Web site. No warranty of any kind, implied, expressed or statutory, including but not limited to the warranties of non-infringement of third party rights, title, merchantability, fitness for a particular purpose and freedom from computer virus, is given with respect to the contents of this Web site or its hyperlinks to other Internet resources. Reference in this Web site to any specific commercial products, processes, or services, or the use of any trade, firm or corporation name is for the information and convenience of the public, and does not constitute endorsement, recommendation, or favoring by company name (2015).

"Linking to Interior Web sites:

Links may be made to this Web site from other personal and organizational Web pages. Company name request that you link to this site rather than downloading portions of it to another Web server, so that our viewers will see our most up-to-date information (2015).

Rights of Publicity, Likeness, etc.:

Certain individuals depicted may claim rights in their likenesses and images. Use of photographs or other materials found on the company name Web site may be subject to these claims. Anyone who intends to use these materials commercially should contact the individuals depicted or their representatives.

Endorsement:

Some of company name Web site Web pages contains links to third party Web sites. The linked sites are not under the control of company name and company name is not responsible for the contents of any linked Web site. These links are provided as a convenience only and shall not be construed as an endorsement of, sponsorship of, or affiliated with the linked Web site by company name.

Website Software and Plug-ins:

It is possible that our site will provide you an opportunity to go to a software manufacturer's Web site so you may download a related plug-in that will enable your browser to show you a part of our Web site. This prompt occurs because your browser needs capabilities provided by these plug-ins. Our system does not read or place anything on your hard drive when recognizing your browser's capabilities. While plug-in(s) may be needed to view or interact with some content, you retain control and choice about conducting the download. At the time that we create and post the web pages that require these software plug-ins for viewing, they are provided by their manufacturer for download and use free of charge. We cannot guarantee, however, that the plug-in will remain free, or that the manufacturer will not collect personally identifying information about you when you elect to download the software from their site. If you choose to visit the manufacturer's Web site to obtain the plug-in, please carefully review their posted policies for details about personal privacy and use of downloaded plug-ins.

Another example can be found on (www.law.freeadvice.com). There, you can learn more about disclaimers specifically for Web sites; however, I've provided some key ideas from the Web site, you should investigate if your clients' Web site does not have these disclaimer key elements already. According to the advice listed on the Web site, all disclaimers should meet these requirements:

- *The material on the Web site is made available with the understanding that you are not engaged in providing professional advice, if you do not have professional credentials to provide such advice*

- *Before relying on material on the Web site, users should independently verify the accuracy, completeness and relevance for their purposes and obtain any appropriate professional advice, if they feel uncomfortable about a Web site and its services and/or products being offered*

- *The material may include opinions, recommendations or other page content from third parties that do not necessarily reflect your views*

- *Links to other Web sites are included for the user's convenience and do not constitute an endorsement of the material on the Web site, or any associated product or service offered by the E-business*[31]

Additionally, the Web site recommends adding a copyright notice that complies with the Digital Millennium Copyright Act (DMCA), which stresses "the Web site and its content are subject to the laws of the United States, that you own the copyright in the material on the site, and which third parties own the copyright to some materials on the site. You will also want to clarify your policy on allowing others to use the material on the site; and what permissions are necessary, etc." [32]

Also, as a construction marketer, you should be aware that ignoring any of the Federal Trade Commission laws, will result in enforcement actions and/or a civil lawsuit filed against the E-business, you work for and/or represent. In fact, the FTC conveys the following penalties on its Web site:

- Orders to cease and desist, with fines up to $11,000 per violation should they occur

- Injunctions by federal district courts, violations of some Commission rules also could result in civil penalties of up to $11,000 per violation; violations of court orders could result in civil or criminal contempt proceedings

- In some instances, refunds to consumers for actual damages in civil lawsuits

In the meantime, you should also be aware that the FCC was successful in establishing the Open Internet Order, in 2010, which has since been revised and entered into effect, May 2014. Under this order, the FCC was able to establish the- *net neutrality*- rules and govern non-discrimination online. Below, I've listed a few details about these regulations:

§8.1 Purpose.

The purpose of this Part is to preserve the Internet as an open platform enabling consumer choice, freedom of expression, end-user control, competition, and the freedom to innovate without permission.

§8.3 Transparency.

A person engaged in the provision of broadband Internet access service shall publicly disclose accurate information regarding the network management practices, performance, and commercial terms of its broadband Internet access services sufficient for consumers to make informed choices regarding use of such services and for content, application, service, and device providers to develop, market, and maintain Internet offerings. (Note: The rule does not require public disclosure of competitively sensitive information or information that would compromise network security or undermine the efficacy of subject to reasonable network management practices.)

§8.5 No Blocking.

A person engaged in the provision of fixed broadband Internet access service, insofar as such person is so engaged, shall not block lawful content, applications, services, or non-harmful devices, subject to reasonable network management.

A person engaged in the provision of mobile broadband Internet access service, insofar as such person is so engaged, shall not block consumers from accessing lawful Web sites, subject to reasonable network management; nor shall such person block applications that compete with the provider's voice or video telephony services, subject to reasonable network management.

§8.7 No Unreasonable Discrimination.

A person engaged in the provision of fixed broadband Internet access service, insofar as such person is so engaged, shall not unreasonably discriminate in transmitting lawful network traffic over a consumer's broadband Internet access service. Reasonable network management shall not constitute unreasonable discrimination. [33]

Please be advised: additional laws have been enacted outside of the United States. For instance, The European Commission of Justice, established the Charter of Fundamental Rights and the Single European Act, which guarantees consumers' fair treatment and a right to redress if something goes wrong. The ECJ also established a consumer protection, which is an essential part of the European Commission's strategic planning. To learn more about this strategic planning and consumer protection, log on to (www.bit.ly/1FY561W).

Meanwhile, in Asia, the increased rate of Internet security privacy right invasions, evoked an online advertising and marketing law to be enacted, by the Hong Kong Privacy Commissioner. The enactment titled *The Personal Data Privacy Ordinance*, was ordained in 2013. In short, it conveys:

- ✓ Individuals must give explicit consent before their data can be used in direct marketing activities (note 'consent' also includes "indication of no objection").
- ✓ Personal data cannot be transferred to third parties for use in direct marketing unless consent is given.
- ✓ An opportunity to opt-out must be clearly available.
- ✓ Marketers' must take specific actions before using personal data in direct marketing in an easily readable and understandable manner. This should include:

- The type of personal data to be used
- The classes of marketing subjects in relation to which the data is to be used
- The classes of persons to which the data is to be provided

To learn more about this enactment, log on to: (www.bit.ly/1wa92gE). Additionally, to help you better define your quest for clarity on international EMarketing laws, you should also log on to (www.en.wikipedia.org) and search: Email Spam Legislations by Country. You can also follow this link (www.bit.ly/1q6HS7L).

Another country that has been influential about EMarketing laws, is Australian. On March 16, 2005, the ACMA was enacted to regulate the compliance of the EMarketing industry, and determined that EMarketers' should operate in compliance with the *Telecommunication Act 1997* and the *Spam Act 2003*. However, on June 5, 2014, the ACMA decided to withdraw its EMarketing Code of Practice. Therefore, before considering launching an EMarketing campaign for a client in Australian, please be sure to review all newly established laws and ordinances'. Using the link provided on the Web page listed at (www.en.wikipedia.org), as pointed out previously, you can click a link that will guide you to the appropriate data Web page- where additional information can be found.

Clearly, it's easy to determine from what I've shared that EMarketing laws have grown substantially around the globe, over the past few years. This is why it's extremely important to know these facts, in order to protect your client from being a victim of circumstances, because he or she had no clue of any of the online advertising and marketing laws in place. Therefore, take the initiative and be the eyes and ears, you were hired to be. Rest assure that if these laws shared in this EMarketing plan exist; there are countless more that have not surfaced as of yet. So utilize all international search engines to search for Internet marketing laws. Doing so may be the best time invested for your clients' long term success, while conducting business online.

SUMMARY

In light of the fact that construction marketing Web site design projects are expensive, complex, and time-consuming undertakings that provide clients' with superior Web pages. Without a sound proof EMarketing plan that's efficient and provides effective methods to achieve optimal performance, in stirring clients' online marketing campaigns towards reaching their goals and objectives; in many instances, such E-businesses remain entangled in endless search engine queries, without much revenue earning in return. After all, in order to enable your client to reach their highest online marketing scale, both nationally and internationally, it is your fiduciary duty to define an EMarketing plan outlined with primary research that's easily understandable.

Additionally, it's also important to always provide clients' with updated legal news about various online E-commerce and EMarketing laws. In fact, just recently as mentioned before: Canada enacted an email marketing law, prohibiting marketers' from sending unsolicited emails to Canadian residence, without prior written consent. And since additional online marketing companies are being established monthly, in one region of the world or another, staying on-top of this important element of Web site design infrastructure, will give your construction marketing agency the leverage it deserves over your competitors.

Now, if your client' has a focus to drive their E-business abroad, internationally; as the EMarketer, it is your duty to also understand international territories, tariffs, treaties, and licensures needed to conduct business in foreign countries. After all, today, leading global construction companies located in China, are now gaining control over countries such as South Africa, because China construction companies are optimizing their knowledge and skills, to beat their U.S. competitors', by large. In fact, research conveyed that conditions of construction contracts commonly used in the United States (AIA-A201) and China (GF-1999-0201) have been analyzed and compared. The findings of this research reveals that the content of sub clauses in AIA-A201 and GF-1999-0201, are different in several ways. These differences may have been caused by cultural, historical, geographical, political, and language variations that exist between the American and Chinese construction markets'. However, understanding these differences will help U.S. companies stay competitive and profitable in, both China and South Africa.[34]

This is why it's essential to utilize the best EMarketing concepts to positions your clients' Web site marketability, as a global construction company. In fact, one specific construction marketing company's president, Kevin Dean, conveyed in an interview that "we have worked with landscaping and construction companies for many years, increasing their businesses via important online strategies like search engine optimization (SEO), pay per click (PPC), social media services, Web site development, mobile solutions, and more. Since then, we've channeled all of our clients' through our main Web site. Though our service information and extensive examples of success stories apply, we felt that a dedicated Web site with Internet Marketing services, products, and results for the landscaping and construction industries, would better serve new prospects. Thus, the new Web site design we implemented better displays our specialized body of work and provides a platform for better communications about the unique solutions we offer."[35]

As a result, due to these findings, resources, and compiled data shared with you in this EMarketing plan, if your clients' are really trying to increase their online presence, boost Web site traffic and/or better promote their services and E- business, in an effort to increase ROI, as well as high tail it to foreign countries' like China's construction companies are doing and build business alliances with long-term investments, such global construction business owners must diminish their personal ideologies about China's business practices, and begin implementing better defined EMarketing concepts that impact growth and development for their E-business. After all, utilizing a company's Web site as a welcome mat for new clients, is the first introduction a Web site visitor sees, when conducting a search engine query for potential business partners.

Moreover, if a company's Web site is not listed in all search engines, globally, that company is already defeating itself on building global alliances and/or increasing the company's online presence. However, as mentioned time and again, with superior guidance from a well- qualified, skilled, and knowledgeable EMarketer, gaining leverage over competitors' isn't as challenging as it would be, if you weren't working with an EMarketer at all. This is the dynamics of EMarketing in a global business environment. An industry of eco-friendly marketability that enables construction marketers' to soar.

Acknowledgements

I'd like to thank, Mr. Gallagher, for extending the help I needed when studying-HTML, Perl™, Apache™, and Java™ Programming.

Next, I'd like to thank, Penn Foster College™, Ashford University Forbes School of Business™, and U.S. Career Institute™ Paralegal Certification program.

Bruce, you stood by me through all of my struggles; thank you.

Mom, thank you for being patient and believing in my vision.

Jay, miss you much!

Nephews and nieces, stay focused and always believe in yourselves; even when everyone else doesn't.

Allen Maintenance®, thank you for giving me a place to work while I was struggling to get through college.

My Spiritual Deity, the one I call upon when I'm weary and troubled by the world around me-Thank you for the will to embrace my inner strengths!

Aunts, uncles, cousins, long lost friends, associates, and extended family: Thank you for walking a short path with me.

Duke, Sebastian, Charity, Chasity, and Dexter: daddy loves you.

WEB SITE DOMAINS

All Web sites shared in this book can be accessed using the links provided:

www.bing.com

www.bitly.com

www.CIA.gov

www.compezy.com

www.constructionwire.com

www.corporationlaw.jds

www.developer.dynamicweb.com

www.enr.construction.com

www.en.wikipedia.org/wiki/Web_banner

www.euromonitor.com

www.expert.gov/tradelenders

www.freeimages.com.uk

www.giveawaytools.com

www.godaddy.com

www.goo.gl

www.industrialwebsearch.com

www.jetro.go.jp/usa

www.lexisnexis.com

www.lycos.com

www.natlawreview.com

www.netcraft.com

www.reputation.com

www.sampleboard.com

www.searchenginecolossus.com

www.skype.com

www.theconstructionindex.co.uk

www.tools.seochat.com/tools/suggest-tool

www.topseos.com/click

www.upra.com

www.webpagesthatsuck.com

www.webs.com

www.wix.com

www.wordstream.com

www.wordtracker.com

www.worldchamber.com

www.worldtrademag.com

www.zanox.com/us

Corporations Mentioned in this EMarketing Plan

Ashford University Forbes School of Business™

Bing™

Construction Law International™

Engineering News Record™

Exposure room™

Facebook™

Forbes™

Forrester Research, Inc. ™

Google™

International Construction Magazine™

Internet Retailer Magazine™

LinkedIn™

Microsoft™

Motion Box™

Open Film™

Penn Foster College™

Podcast™

Silverstein Properties™

Target Magazine™

Twitter™

U.S. Career Institute™

Viemo™

Website Magazine™

Webs.com™

Windows 8™

Wix.com™

Yahoo! ™

YouTube™

List of Social Media Networks Listed in This Book

AltaVista®

Amazon®

Asian Avenue®

A Small World®

Auction Web®

Baidu®

Biip.no®

Drop Box®

Elixio®

Facebook®

Flikr®

LinkedIn®

Pinterest®

Reddit®

Tumblr®

Twitter®

WordPress®

Yandex®

YouTube®

REFERENCE

1 Chaffey, D. & Smith, P.R. 2008. EMarketing Excellence: *"Planning & Optimizing Your Digital Marketing."* Butterworth-Heineman, Oxford, UK. p.13

2 Hayes, Steven. 2013. *"In Africa, U.S. Businesses Are Losing out to China."* U.S. News. August, 2014, [Web file]. Retrieved from: http://www.usnews.com/opinion/blogs/world-report/2013/02/08/in-africa-us-businesses-are-losing-out-to-china

3 Eryn, Travis. 2014. *Ehow.com.* August, 2014, [Web file]. Retrieved from: http://www.ehow.com/info_7981853_corporate-loss-due-poor-communication.html

4 Parson, Ellen. 2005. *ECMWEB.com.* August, 2014, [Web file]. Retrieved from: http://ecmweb.com/content/construction-industrys-ethical-dilemma

5 Kumar, M. S., & Singh, M. P. 2014. *"Empirical Analysis of Ethical issue of Privacy in E-Marketing."* Bridgepoint Education, Inc., New York, NY, p. 1

6 OYEWOBI, L.O., GANIYU, O. B., OKE, A. A. W OLA-AWO, SHITTU, A. A. 2011. *"Journal of Sustainable Development."* August, 2014. [Web file]. Retrieved from: http://www.ccsenet.org/journal/index.php/jsd/article/view/10287

7 Schneider, G. 2009. *"Electronic Ecommerce."* Boston, Massa chutes. p. 66

8 Nagunwa, T. 2014. "*The Society of Digital Information and Wireless Communications.*" September 2014. [Web file]. Retrieved from: http://sdiwc.net/digital-library/behind-identity-theft-and-fraud-in-cyberspace-the-current-landscape-of-phishing-vectors

9 Pantov, V. 2013. *"The Prevention of Cybersquatting in Europe: Diverging Approaches and Prospects for Harmonization. MIPLC Thesis Series (2012/13)".* 11 September 2014. [Web file]. Retrieved from: http://papers.ssrn.com/sol3/papers.cfm?abstract_id=2427582

10 Dusto, A. 2013. Internet Retailer: "*Global E-commerce tops $1 trillion in 2012.*" Chicago, IL. September, 2014. [Web file]. Retrieved from: http://www.internetretailer.com/2013/02/05/global-e-commerce-tops-1-trillion-2012

11 Netcraft.com. 2014. Internet Live Stats: "*Total Number of Web sites, World Wide Web Association.*" September, 2014. [Web file]. Retrieved from: http://www.internetlivestats.com/total-number-of-websites/

12 Cottrell, M.L.2011. HTML & XHTML Demystified: "*Hard Stuff Made Easy.*" McGraw Hill, New York, NY. p.4

13 Gehl, D. 2009. Entreprenuer.com. *"Grab Customers with Long-Tail Keywords."* 12 September 2014. [Web file]. Retrieved from: http://www.entrepreneur.com/article/201070

14 International Construction. 23 November 2014. [Web file]. Retrieved from: https://itunes.apple.com/us/app/international-construction/id571654112?mt=8

15 UPS Store.com. 2014. UPS: "*How to Use Social Media Marketing To Market Your Construction Business.*" 12 September 2014. [Web file]. Retrieved from: http://smallbiz.theupsstore.com/blog/small-business-blog/2012/10/17/how-to-use-social-media

16 Cateora, P., Gilly, M. & Graham, J. 2011. *International Marketing*. McGraw-Hill Irwin, Boston, MA, p.130

17 Central Intelligence Agency.gov. 2014. The World Fact Book: *"Country Comparison Internet Users."* September, 2014. [Web file]. Retrieved from: https://www.cia.gov/library/publications/the-world-factbook/rankorder/2153rank.html

18 Munro, J. 2003. COMMUNICATION PROTECTOR: "*FIREWALLS". PC Magazine*, *22*(17), 87

19 Freed, L. (1999). Proxy Server Solution. *PC Magazine*, *18*(5), 76.

20 Nagar, V., & Singh, I. (2003). *U.S. Patent No. 6,604,143*. Washington, DC: U.S. Patent and Trademark Office.

21 Technet.Microsoft.com, (2014). TechNet: Authentication Protocol Overview. Accessed October, 2014. [Web file]. Retrieved from: http://technet.microsoft.com/en-us/library/cc739177 (v=WS.10).aspx

22 Geier, Eric, (2012.)PC World.com: How to Encrypt your Email. Accessed October, 2014. [Web file]. Retrieved from: http://www.pcworld.com/article/254338/how_to_encrypt_your_email.html

23 Microsoft.com. 2014. "*Safe and Security: 11 Steps for Social Networking Security.*" October, 2014. [Web file]. Retrieved from: http://www.microsoft.com/security/online-privacy/social-networking.aspx

24 Microsoft.com. 2014. "*Cyber Trust Blog: Be Careful With Social Networking Sites, Especially At Work.*" October, 2014. [Web file]. Retrieved from: http://blogs.microsoft.com/cybertrust/2008/09/02/be-careful-with-social-networking-sites-especially-at-work

25 Nolta, Brandon. 2014. "*Penn Foster College Student Study Guide: Internet Security.*" Scranton, PA. p. 74

26 Ranker.com. 2014. "*Best Construction Companies World Wide.*" 17 October, 2014. [Web file]. Retrieved from: http://www.ranker.com/list/construction-companies/reference

27 Yale.edu. 2014. "*Search Services: Optimizing Your Web Content for Search Visibility.*" 29 October 2014. [Web file]. Retrieved from: http://www.yale.edu/web/search/web-search-optimization.html

28 Federal Trade Commission, 2000. "*Bureau of Consumer Protection: Advertising and Marketing Laws.*" 6 December 2014. [Web file]. Retrieved from: http://business.ftc.gov/documents/bus28-advertising-and-marketing-internet-rules-road

29 The U.S. Department of the Interior, 2014. "*Copyrights, Restrictions, and Permissions*." 6 December 2014. [Web file]. Retrieved from: http://www.doi.gov/copyright.cfm

30 Lawfreeadvice.com. 2014. Websites: "*Writing the Disclaimers and Copyright Notices*." 6 December 2014. [Web file]. Retrieved from: http://law.freeadvice.com/intellectual_property/computer_law/website-disclaimers-copyright-notices.htm

31 Ibid.

32 en.wikipedia.org. 2014. FCC Open Internet Order 2010: Rules. 6 December 2014. [Web file]. Retrieved from: http://en.wikipedia.org/wiki/FCC_Open_Internet_Order_2010#Rules

33 Chui, K., & Bai, Y. (2010). Comparison of Contract General Conditions between United States and China. Journal of Architectural Engineering, 16(4), 119-125. Doi: 10. 1061/ (ASCE) AE. 1943-5568.0000020

34 PRweb.com. 2014. "*New Website Launched for Landscaping and Construction Companies' Online Marketing Needs.*" 4 January, 2014. [Web file]. Retrieved from: http:// www.PRWeb.com (USA).

BIBLIOGRAPHIES

Cateora, P., Gilly, M. & Graham, J., *International Marketing, 15th edition,* New York, N.Y.: McGraw-Hill Irwin (2011); 130 p.

Chaffey, D. & Smith, P.R. *EMarketing Excellence*: *Planning & Optimizing Your Digital Marketing*, 3rd. edition Oxford, UK: Butterworth-Heineman (2008); 13 p.

Cottrell, M.L. *HTML & XHTML Demystified*: *Hard Stuff Made Easy, 2nd edition*, New York, N.Y.: McGraw-Hill Irwin (2011); 4 p.

GLOSSARY

A

Alternative Dispute Resolution Systems- known as external dispute resolution in some countries, specifically Australia. Seemingly, it includes dispute resolution processes and techniques, which act as a means for non-agreeable parties to come to some agreement without litigation.

Affiliate Marketing-a performance based marketing concept shared between B2B; which a sponsoring E-business extends payment to a hosting E-business owner, who post pay per click advertisements on their Web site for payment and traffic flow exchange.

Authentication List-

Auto-Responders-an email computer program that sends an automatic message response programmed by the sender.

C

Civil law- derived from Roman law and found in Germany, Japan, France, and non-Islamic and non-Marxist Countries.

Common law-refers to judge-made (rather than legislature made) law or to law that had its origin in England and grew from ever-changing custom. And tradition (rather than king-made law).

Cybersquatting-the use of commercial trademarked corporate domain names without permission, with hopes of selling them at a higher price.

D

Domain Name-compiled of several components, domain name is the name of a Web site.

F

Filter Servlet-mapped to a URL and then mapped to a URL pattern.

Firewall- a software program designed to block unauthorized access to a computer system database and/or hard drive.

H

HTML- (Hyper Text Markup Language) defines the text, font, colors, images, and actions within the Web pages of a World Wide Web site.

HTTPS- a sublayer under HTML layers, which enables Security Socket Layers, to protect Web site Web pages.

I

Islamic Law-the law according to Muslim faith; known as the Sharia law.

J

Java-a computer programming language that can be used on any computer.

K

Kerberos V5 Authentication-provides a mechanism for authentication between a client and server or servers.

Keyword Tracker-keywords used in HTML Meta tag codes to enhance search engine registry ranking.

L

Long Tail Keyword Phrases-two to five terms used to conduct a distinct search engine query.

M

Malware-software that enters a computer system without the user's knowledge or consent and then performs an unwanted – and usually harmful-action.

Meta tags-used to hold information about a Web page; will not be displayed on the screen.

N

NTTP News-(Network News Protocol) an application used for transmitting Usenet news articles between news servers.

P

Page-content hijacking-stealing Web site page content and applying that page content to another Web site, without the original Web site owner's permission.

Passport Authentication-used on public Web sites by many email users; identifies a single user's email address.

Pay-Per-Click- paid Internet advertising banners that enable Web site users to click and view advertised data.

Phishing Emails-email fraud format used by criminals to evoke email viewers to share personal data such as home address, bank data and/or credit card data.

Podcast-digital audio file downloaded and uploaded to computer or portable media player.

Point to Point Protocol-data link used to connect two nodes; can enable transmission encryption.

POP3-protocol used for downloading emails on a computer on the server of an Internet protocol.

Proxy Server-a server that acts as a mediator server for clients seeking resources from other servers.

R

Res Judicata- a matter adjudicated within a competent court that may not be pursued further by either party.

S

Security Socket Layer- (SSL) standard encryption technology used to secure links shared between Web server and Web browsers.

Short Tail Keyword Phrases-one or two words used to conduct a search engine query.

Spear Phishing-fraudulent email that duplicates a business you are familiar with. Used by criminals to gain data to hack sensitive data, such as bank, credit card, and social security numbers.

SMTP Email-(Simple Mail Transfer Protocol) standard for email transmission; by default, uses TCP port 25.

Sui Generis ADR's- unique.

SWOT Analysis-used by organization to determine a company's strengths, weaknesses, opportunities, and threats. Often used by Internet Marketer's, EMarketer's, and Digital Media Marketer's.

T

Top Level Domains-the highest domain name level in the domain name hierarchical Domain Name System.

Transport Layer Security-(TLS) cryptographic protocol used to provide communication over the Internet.

Typography-style and printed matter, such as arranging data.

U

Uniform Domain Name Dispute Resolution Policy-(UDRP) established by Internet Corporation for Assigned Names and Numbers (ICAN) for the resolution of disputes regarding the registration of domain names.

Unique Host Name-related links of information, names, and terms.

Universal Resource Locator- (URL) a string of specific characters used to define a Web site address.

W

WAN Connection-consists of two or more local-area network (LAN) and spans a large geographical region.

Web Crawlers- a software program or automated script used to browse in a methodical automated manner.

Web Search Ability- advertising and marketing methods used for Internet marketing search engine ranking enhancement.

Web Spiders- are used to feed pages to search engines.

www.ingramcontent.com/pod-product-compliance
Ingram Content Group UK Ltd.
Pitfield, Milton Keynes, MK11 3LW, UK
UKHW020209290926
15470UKWH00001B/91